Drawing & Painting
Portraits

John Devane

Quantum
Books

A QUANTUM BOOK

This book is produced by
Quantum Publishing Ltd.
6 Blundell Street
London N7 9BH

ISBN 1-86160-593-5

QUMPDP

Filmset by QV Typesetting Limited, London
Origination by
Hong Kong Graphic Arts Service Centre Limited,
Hong Kong

Printed in Singapore by
Star Standard Industries (Pte) Ltd.

Quarto would like to extend special thanks to Helen
Begley, Jane Cross, Colette Koo, Adebayo Odofin,
Hugh Sanders.

CONTENTS

INTRODUCTION

The sheer number and variety of portraits drawn and painted over the centuries provides a fascinating source of imagery, lending insights into changing social conventions and tastes and bringing the past to life. They bear witness to artists' continuing attempts to depict the complexity and uniqueness of the human character and temperament. While portraits are intended to display specific features or reveal the character of an individual, they often, perhaps surprisingly, reveal as much about the artist and the artist's relationship with the subject. The conflict created between the intention, to depict an individual, and the result, which often implies a great deal more, is of lasting interest to artist and layman alike.

The existence of figurative sketches on cave walls drawn by the people of the Ice Age *c* 15,000 BC, suggests that it is almost instinctive for human beings to want to represent themselves. These drawings are not portraits but pictures of anonymous figures and animals illustrated in lively, stylized form. By comparison, portraits as they are understood today have existed as an art form for the relatively short period of about two and a half thousand years, and emerged in the type of civilization in which there was a need to celebrate or commemorate individuality.

Thus portraiture has passed in and out of favour. In the Middle Ages, for instance, portraiture hardly existed because works of art were created only for the glorification of God. The English *Wilton Diptych* includes a picture of King Richard II (1367 - 1400) kneeling before the Virgin; the King is only identifiable by the hart emblems on his cloak. Both before and after that, the intention of much portraiture in the Western world has been to present not individual character but a person in his or her social, political or religious role, so celebrating status or riches. Sometimes portraits have been, and are, set within mythological or historical compositions for similar reasons. However, it may be seen that during and since the Renaissance, two different and very general approaches to the art of portraiture have run parallel. The presentation of the actual personality of the subjects has been important for some artists, sometimes at the expense of their reputations and patrons' support in the form of commissions. Artists painting good likenesses of patrons for specific occasions or in robes of office have usually been able to earn a living, while artists painting for personal interest or in the pursuit of truth have not.

If a portrait is described as a 'good likeness', the implication is that the sum of the features is instantly recognizable to anyone who has met or seen the subject, and it is generally assumed that all the greatest portrait painters were able to oblige their patrons with such a likeness. However, alone, the reproduction of features does not necessarily reveal a great deal about the subject, and certainly has nothing to do with the

quality of the painting. The warm response of viewers looking at portraits by Old Masters — portraits of men and women unknown to them — is often provoked by the perception of a kind of sympathy or understanding existing between sitter and artist. Some great artists have been able to reveal this kind of true feeling without losing the respect of their patrons.

Because portraits necessarily record how the artist sees the subject, they cannot be truly objective. In painting one face, the artist records a

ABOVE **Portrait of a Lady,** Bartholomeus van der Helst. (1613 - 70). This unusual portrait, with its black-on-black effect, was painted by Amsterdam's leading portrait painter of the mid-seventeenth century. He has ensured the unity of the painting by matching the lady's dark eyes and strong pale face to the starkly contrasting blacks and whites of the whole. The dress is in fact a dark blue-black, rich in both colour and texture, while it is toned against a brown-black background. The lace and pearls are painted in intricate detail to indicate the subject's wealth, and their blue whites contrast with the warmer whites of her skin.

LEFT **Portrait of a Girl**,
Domenico Ghirlandaio (c 1448
- 94). This portrait has been
attributed by some to the
hand of Sebastiano Mainardi
(active 1493 - d 1513), who
worked in the studio of
Ghirlandaio, and the truth
remains a mystery. Whoever
the artist was, the quiet
beauty of this portrait bears
witness to a mastery of
naturalistic paint effects. The
picture is unified by the use
of complementary greens and
reds in the dress, the
necklace, the hair decoration
and the rosiness of the girl's
lips. Her bearing, high
forehead and flaxen hair,
combined with her downcast
eyes, make a subtle
statement on the idealistic
modesty of the young
Renaissance woman.

Self-portraits by Rembrandt
In these self-portraits, just three of the dozens he painted, Rembrandt recorded his psychological and physical changes with a characteristic mastery of the medium combined with acute self-awareness. Self-portraits demand a peculiar two-fold understanding. Using a mirror and painting the reflected image, the artist is treating his own face as if it belonged to another person; simultaneously he is privileged with a depth of self-knowledge. This conflict can cause ambiguity in the painting, certainly not aided by the difficulty of extricating mistaken preconceptions which would hinder a truthful picture. The character of the artist is revealed to an extent by the changing painting style. At ages 34, 53 and 63, these portraits show the development of Rembrandt's techniques while his face aged. In the first he is a successful young painter, much in demand. During the 1640s, in other works, he started concentrating on the inner character or spirituality of his subjects. By the time he was 53, his wife had died and he was bankrupt, and the sadness caused him to paint energetically for himself. The third portrait reveals the face of disillusion. The blurred paint betrays an acceptance of his life's tragedies.

two-way reaction. Some portraits describe the sympathy between the painter and the person being painted; others, not necessarily less good, display a formality, and some a satirical or otherwise harsh response. Other reasons for the necessary subjectivity of a portrait exist. The artist may feel that the character of the subject could be enhanced by a certain background or the inclusion of objects, which would provide hints as to the situation or interests of the subject. A great deal of realism has been employed by many portraitists, others have presented their subjects within a disconnected or abstracted vision. These comparisons illustrate differences in artists' intentions, as prompted by the personality of the subject. They also illustrate how the background and character of the artist may to some extent be revealed.

In some portraits, the interaction between artist and sitter is displayed more overtly than in the implied mood or intention. In attempting to portray an individual realistically, some artists involuntarily include their own physical characteristics. As Leonardo da Vinci (1452 - 1519) wrote in his *Treatise on Painting*: '. . . If you were ugly, you would select faces that are not beautiful and you would paint ugly faces, as do many painters, whose painted figures often resemble that of their master.' It is interesting to compare the portraits by Rembrandt van Rijn (1606 - 69), for example, with his many self-portraits. Hardly a year went by when he did not commit his own features to canvas, and it becomes apparent that in many of his portraits of others there is a resemblance to his own features. These similarities cannot simply be ac-

counted for by the use of immediate family as models. Often the resemblance is not only in the face but concerns the body as a whole.

In these terms, the most revealing type of portrait might be said to be the self-portrait, in which inner and outer characteristics can be portrayed without the inhibiting attempt to come to terms with the separateness of another person. Painting a self-portrait could be considered as the ultimate attempt to combine the inner and outer self. At the same time, the discipline enables the artist to become increasingly aware of the complexity involved in observing features and expressions and committing them to canvas or paper. Rembrandt's memorable self-portraits amount to a visual graph of the inevitable ageing process.

The Spanish painter Velasquez (1599-1660),

FAR LEFT **Las Meninas (The Maids of Honour)**, Diego Velasquez. The artist may have used a mirror to paint this group portrait, which includes himself, and painted the reflection, not reality. However, to be truthful to the mirror reflection, he would have had to paint the back views of the King and Queen of Spain (who appear in a mirror on the wall behind) and their bodies would have blocked almost everything else from view. In reality they probably did not stand in front of the group; in other words, in reality, the people at the centre of the idea were not there.

LEFT **A Bar at the Folies Bergère**, Edouard Manet. From the mirror reflection it is evident that the girl is taking an order, perhaps from the artist. The implication of life connected with it but going on outside it brings the picture alive.

BELOW One of **A Series of Pictures of Beauties Making Up**, Kitagawa Utamaro. This wood-block print exploits the mirror reflection to make a simple statement on the grace and beauty of a Japanese lady.

unlike his contemporary Rembrandt, did not display any desire to produce self-portraits except in *Las Meninas* (*The Maids of Honour*), which he painted late in life. In this picture, he included a self-portrait which was in fact an image of the artist as seen by others. The painting is a comment about the painting of portraits. The actual subjects of the portrait within the whole group — the King and Queen of Spain — are not in the picture except in reflection. The viewer becomes the subject, standing in the imaginary position of the royal couple. In this visual paradox, Velasquez seems to be confronting the nature of reality, forcing the viewer to an awareness of the deception caused by an acceptance of illusion.

The use of realism in painting is an attempt to create an illusion. The artist is presenting a picture as if it is part of the actual world, as if the viewer were looking through a window onto the presented scene. Realism in painting may be described as the representation of the natural world in as generally recognizable a way as possible using perspective and tone and other painterly devices. As realism became accepted in the Western world, its aims became confused and this resulted in a common misconception that the sole purpose of painting was to mimic the natural world. The importance attached to this realism is essentially a Western dilemma. Eastern cultures have always remained aware of the distinction between the visual world and the world of artifice that includes the flat surface of a painting. The Eastern point of view is reinforced in the way that the Western vision of reality, as presented on canvas or paper, has changed over the centuries. This in itself is further proof of the impossibility of an objective portrait. Art is not life; the fascination of painting and drawing is in the revelation of personal visions.

Fifteenth-century technical innovations like the use of oil paint in some respects impinged on the subtlety with which earlier European artists combined an acute awareness of visual phenomena with an understanding of a painting as a separate entity in two dimensions. The twentieth-century awareness of reality as seen through the camera lens has hindered an understanding of that subtlety, and accounts for much of the hostility attached to the more abstract developments in painting that do not accord with a naturalistic view. It is important to be aware of the fact that all painting is illusion. Simultaneously, however, in portraiture, a degree of realism is required in order to capture the uniqueness of the individual.

THE ART OF PORTRAITURE

Elements of realism in the representation of the human figure and face are evident in art since the Classical age, and it is obvious that human beings have changed little over the centuries. However, between the age of Antiquity and the present day, the roles of artist and patron have completely changed. No longer needing to curry favour with patrons or carry out precise directions, artists have achieved a status that has enabled them to choose how to depict their subjects and sometimes even to choose the subjects themselves. This survey of the development of portraiture attempts to define some of the reasons for that change and how they have affected the art itself, by considering artists from different Western centres of civilization and charting a path in connection with the economic and social progress of the different societies.

Any attempt to explore the history of portraiture will result in a study of some of the greatest artists that have ever lived. However, it is not true to say that the art of portraiture began when human beings first began to depict others. Art invariably reflects the attitudes of the society from which it emerges so the need to paint portraits reflects a society that attaches importance to a belief in individuality. The Ancient Greeks are renowned for remarkable images of idealized human beings, their gods and goddesses being immortalized as perfect beings in marble and stone. The portrait occupied a minor position in Greek society because their philosophical ideals led them to depict people in universal terms. The portrait could only emerge in a society where a uniqueness of character and an acknowledgement of imperfections could be reflected.

One of the earliest forms of portraiture, from the sixth century BC, commemorated not the living but the dead, and emerged in north-central Italy in the form of death masks. The Etruscans had a profound fear of dying, and the significance that they attached to it promoted a fashion for posthumous portraits that, in their eyes, enabled the deceased to pass safely into the afterlife. A similar form of portrait emerged in Egypt with the Greek settlers who adopted the native custom of mummification. They attained a high degree of realism in portraits that were usually painted in wax on cypress-wood panels.

Rome had become the centre of the ancient world by the second century BC, and the consequent shift in wealth and patronage directly contributed to developments in portraiture. Enthralled by the splendours of their conquests, the Romans enlisted the talents of Greek artists to celebrate their status and bequeath their features to posterity. The impersonal beauty of Greek art surrendered to the more egotistical requirements of the Romans. An example of the compromise that occurred is apparent when a portrait image on a medal of the first Roman Emperor, Augustus (27BC - AD14) is compared with a written account of his appearance. Suetonius, the biographer of Augustus, wrote:

RIGHT **Portrait of a Man and Wife.** This expressive double funeral portrait was painted in wax on a cypress-wood panel. Previously, the Greeks had tended to idealize the human form in sculpture and portraits, but by the time of Alexander the Great, the Greek artists, employed by Romans, began to portray their subjects with a little more honesty, particularly in Pompeii. This portrait shows traces of idealization but the features, the particular shapes of the noses and chins, seem realistic and individual.

BELOW This Roman coin, although battered around the edges, retains a bold image of the Emperor, carefully modelled to describe specific features such as the nose, the shape of the mouth, the moustache and beard. The profile shows surprising realism, particularly in comparison with later English coins of the Middle Ages, which were simple and stylized in comparison. The spiked crown, hair and robes display marked attention to detail.

'He did not dress extravagantly and cared so little about his hair...was rather short, but had well proportioned limbs ... he sometimes limped and suffered generally from a weak constitution.' The portrait, however, reveals how the Emperor wished to look and be remembered and little of his actual appearance or character.

Roman heads probably resembled particular individuals with reasonable accuracy, yet the figures often conformed to an ideal conception — the idea inherited from the Greeks. In extreme examples of imperial portraiture, the god-like image is substantiated by a disproportionately large torso beneath the head. The irreconcilable union of Roman vanity and Greek perfection sometimes resulted in absurdity.

Roman portraiture existed in a stable, affluent society, but as the civilization collapsed so the tradition declined. It was only with the dawn of the Renaissance that portraiture began to revive. Italy became the home of a resurgence of interest in individuals partly because the princes of prosperous Italian cities could afford to commemorate themselves and their riches, and partly because of the area's crucial connection with the ancient civilization. It was a time when human curiosity about the world resulted in a desire for rational explanations. An attitude of intellectual enquiry emerged from the deeply rooted theological concerns of the Middle Ages. The Italian philosophers and artists rediscovered the powerful classical ideals of perspective and proportion and other mathematical manifestations of an ordered world; they were the first to forward the idea that human beings are an inherent part of nature, and everything conforms to a potentially perfect unity. The role of artists changed during the High Renaissance: they emerged as having rationales of their own instead of being seen as artisans or craftsmen dependent on manual dexterity, which was the Greek view.

LEFT **Battista Sforza**, Piero della Francesca. One side of a diptych, this portrait is of the wife of Federico da Montefeltro, the Duke of Urbino, who not surprisingly appears, facing her, on the other. Working in Italy during the fifteenth century, Piero della Francesca usually painted in fresco or tempera and imbued his art with a mathematical harmony and spiritual calm. This precise profile of the Duchess is reminiscent of the profile heads on coins and medals made during the Roman times.

The profile, which had adorned medals and coins for centuries, was adopted in painting in the late thirteenth century. However, despite the fact that it was capable of revealing both physical and psychological characteristics, it began to be considered unrealistic and static when included in early Florentine religious paintings. With the increasing Renaissance interest in solid volume came the more fashionable three-quarter view of the face. The discovery of perspective enabled artists to depict a three-dimensional view of the world as seen from a fixed point. For the first time, figures and forms began to be organized in space in such a way that they decreased in size as they receded from the picture plane.

Giotto di Bondone (c 1267 - 1337) is generally considered to be the first originally creative artist in Western painting. *The Annunciation to St Anne* includes an unforgettable image of a servant girl. Although this is not a portrait in the strict sense, it amply displays the artist's concern with a revolutionary form of depiction. The girl is not a purely religious figure, but is sitting at her work, and the three-quarter view of her face seems solid and well formed. Giotto was not presenting a particular individual, but a surprisingly naturalistic picture of a girl who may or may not have lived.

As patrons of the arts began to want to surround themselves not just with the products of the cultural achievement but with images of themselves, the popularity of the portrait increased. It is interesting to see how the Italian representations of figures differed from the northern European. Compared to the mathematical precision of southern works, portraitists from The Netherlands and Flanders tended towards a greater naturalism in their paintings at the expense of unity and harmony. The term 'Gothic' was originally a pejorative description made by the Italian Humanists and applied to the art produced from the early twelfth century to the first half of the sixteenth century in northern Europe. However, the Italians were prepared to concede that in some areas the northern Europeans were superior, and there was a surprising interaction between the two parts of Europe. In 1456, the Italian scholar Bartolomeo Fazio paid a tribute to Jan van Eyck (active 1422 - d 1441) when he acknowledged his ability and remarkable technical advances and even considered him a leading painter of the time.

Jan van Eyck is often credited with the invention of oil paint. The truth of this claim is difficult to ascertain, however, it is certain that he perfected an oil medium and varnish that has enabled the brilliance of his colours to survive to this day. A painting that typifies his achievement is the wedding portrait of Giovanni Arnolfini and Giovanna Cenami, the children of wealthy Italian merchants established in Bruges, which was finished in 1434. The serene physiognomy exemplifies the style of northern European paint-

ing at that time, but despite the microscopic attention given to surfaces and the realistic feeling of light and space, the actual poses of the figures are rooted in earlier Gothic sculpture. The statuesque couple join hands with a ceremonial calmness and gaze out from their bedchamber while the spectator replaces the original witnesses to the marriage vows.

Petrus Christus (active 1442? - d 1472/73) emerged as the major painter in Bruges after van Eyck's death. Although much of his work is derivative, *Portrait of a Girl*, generally considered to be Lady Talbot, is both beautiful and strikingly individual. The fascination that this tiny

ABOVE **Portrait of a Girl,** Petrus Christus. The inquisitive yet wary air of this young girl has been captured by the Netherlandish artist to create a beautiful and, at the same time, disturbing portrait. Her shyness is endearing because her expression of self-assurance is an attempt to deny it. Christus' mastery of the oil medium allowed him to reveal a distinct personality behind the youthful gaze.

RIGHT **Portrait of a Man,** Antonello da Messina. This confident work is traditionally considered to be a self-portrait, probably painted in 1475. Originally the eyes were painted looking the other way, but in the final version the subject is staring at the spectator so forcing a direct confrontation and demanding a response. The Flemish style of the three-quarter view was to have an important influence.

painting exerts is partly due to the expression on the child-like face. Because of the fashionably plucked eyebrows and high forehead, the oval purity of the face becomes apparent. The gentle facial contours are smooth, and yet any mask-like resemblance is relieved by the penetrating stare of the slightly slanting eyes.

By contrast, in many examples of Flemish portraiture the subject appears to be unaware of the artist's presence or self-absorbed and deep in prayer. The portraits by Rogier van der Weyden (c 1400 - 64) usually follow this pattern, and his *Portrait of a Lady*, although similar in posture and facial type, is quite different in feeling from the almost provocative countenance of the girl by Petrus Christus. The direct confrontation between Lady Talbot, if it is she, and the artist is apparent, despite the stiffly encased little body, and reveals a particular person with a credible human presence.

By comparing the works of Flemish and Italian painters during the fifteenth century it is possible to detect the overlap of influence that occurred. The lessons learned from van Eyck are evident in the work of Antonello da Messina (c 1430 - 79), who was probably the most important southern Italian painter at the time and certainly responsible for the Italian involvement with oil paint. Antonello adopted the Flemish love of detail but managed to incorporate it into a breadth and harmony of design that is purely Italian. His portraits probably influenced Giovanni Bellini (1430/40 - 1516) and many other painters who acquired a knowledge of Flemish paintings without actually seeing them.

As portraits became fashionable, artists were required to expand their formal repertoire. Hans Memling (1430/5 - 94), whose art is purely Netherlandish, found favour with Italian clients by combining portraiture with a glimpse of landscape. By comparison, the work of Piero della Francesca (1410/20 - 92) embodies all the Renaissance ideals: it combines realistic representation held in check by mathematical considerations of formal relationships. For Memling landscape provided an interesting foil to figures; Piero was fundamentally prepoccupied with landscape as the space human beings occupy. 'Renaissance man' is usually depicted as being at one with the natural world, and from Giotto onwards most religious depictions occur in the open air, in contrast to the closeted world favoured by the Flemish painters.

One of the most talented of early Flemish painters after van Eyck to influence Florentine painters was Hugo van der Goes (active c 1467 -82). Tommaso Portinari, an agent for the House of Medici in Bruges, commissioned an altar painting by him which was sent to Florence on completion. This provided the Italians with a first-hand glimpse of a remarkable oil painting. Apart from the originality of its composition and large scale, which was unusual for a Flemish artist of this time, it illustrated a virtuoso

performance of a complex religious scene with landscape in the background and life-size portraits of shepherds and children flanking the centre picture. Although large-scale frescos were commonplace, an oil painting of such complexity as *The Portinari Altarpiece* was a great achievement.

The leading French painter of the fifteenth century was Jean Fouquet (*c* 1420 - *c* 1481). He was certainly influenced by the new Renaissance ideas, especially the desire to depict tangible volume. As with Hugo van der Goes, his most powerful picture is a strange diptych, the *Diptych of Melun,* combining a religious scene with portraiture. In the lefthand panel his patron Etienne Chevalier, Chancellor of France, is seen kneeling beside an enigmatic image of St Stephen. A grasp of reality is confirmed by the implied weight of a book St Stephen is holding; its volume is understood and it occupies a three-dimensional space. The slight tilt of St Stephen's head and the fact that it is seen from below, contrasts and breaks the monotony of what might have been a repetition of the more upright posture of Chevalier. Despite St Stephen's neatly trimmed hair, his wrinkled skin and expression are naturalistically represented. The opposite panel of the diptych is more overtly Gothic in appearance. Peculiar red cherubs surround the stiff Madonna figure, and the bizarre format of the picture is accentuated by speculation that the Madonna is also a portrait of Chevalier's mistress.

As Renaissance ideas evolved and spread through Europe, the importance of the artist as an individual became more apparent. With the passage of time, the myth surrounding an artist grows, and sometimes less attention is focused on the subject than on the painter. The name of Leonardo da Vinci resounds through history. Apart from epitomizing the Renaissance ideal, Leonardo's relatively small output of paintings seems to endorse the mystery of his genius. The *Mona Lisa*, perhaps the best-known portrait ever to be painted, is shrouded in mystery, partly because of the awe generated by the mastery of its creator and partly because so little is known about its origin. The wooden panel is unsigned

FAR LEFT AND LEFT **The Portinari Altarpiece,** Hugo van der Goes. The Flemish artist was commissioned by Tommaso Portinari, the Medici representative at Bruges, to paint a large-scale altarpiece for the church of the Hospital of Sta Maria Nuova in Florence. When displayed, in about 1476, the proficient handling of oil paint and mastery of design surprised and pleased the Italians, who adopted oil techniques later than the northern Europeans. These two side-panels of the triptych show the donor and his family with their patron saints standing behind. The volumes and textures of the clothing are described richly yet delicately; similarly the women's jewellery and the hands of the children are painted in minute detail. The activity of the background figures adds life and vigour to these fine paintings.

and undated, and there are no records of payment, suggesting that it was not a commissioned work, nor any information that could shed light on its intended owner. There are no drawings by Leonardo that could be interpreted as preparatory studies and there is some speculation about the actual identity of the subject.

The lack of information on the *Mona Lisa* is all the more surprising in the light of the visual clues given by Leonardo in the majority of his paintings. His iconographical references, which have been considered in depth by various critics, reveal specific information about the sitters. In the portrait *Ginevra de' Benci*, for instance, the foliage of juniper amid the surrounding landscape can be interpreted as a visual pun on the woman's name, *ginevra* meaning juniper in early Italian dialects. Another portrait entitled *Lady with an Ermine* represents Cecilia Gallerani, the mistress of Il Moro whose emblem included the ermine. The effects of juxtaposing the woman and the animal were certainly calculated by Leonardo, and even without knowledge of the emblematic association, the echoes provide a disturbing note to what might otherwise have been a traditional portrait. The unblinking stare of the ermine is matched by the sharp delineation of the woman's features, and the position of her beautifully drawn hand is repeated in the position of the animal's claw. Both these portraits differ considerably from the *Mona Lisa*. Not only do they definitely represent particular individuals, they also display hairstyles and clothing which were typical of contemporary fashion. By comparison, the *Mona Lisa*, devoid of jewellery and visual clues, seems timeless.

It has been suggested that the *Mona Lisa* is a composite portrait painted over a number of years and perhaps fusing together the images of more than one model. On a purely technical level, the paintwork has an organic quality achieved by imperceptible layers of transparent paint blended without a linear emphasis on contour. The early years of Leonardo's work on the *Mona Lisa* coincided with a period of anatomical study in Florence. Between 1503 and 1506 he lived in the Hospital of Santa Maria Nuova, and the subsequent knowlege gained must have affected the course of his painting. The degree of realism attained was the result of an increased awareness of the structures beneath the skin. Most medieval doctrines encouraged the belief that the universe could only be understood spiritually, but Leonardo believed knowledge to be based on an objective understanding of experiences combined with mathematical reasoning. In his own writings, he expressed contempt for the aristocracy of Florence who based their intellectual superiority on a tradition of acquired knowledge and relied on memory rather than natural intelligence.

Leonardo considered the *Mona Lisa* important enough to accompany him on his travels,

and even in an unfinished state it exerted considerable influence over the fashion for single figure portraiture. It is almost certain that Raphael (1483 - 1520) saw the picture, and now, more than ever, the enigmatic presence of the *Mona Lisa* continues to attract speculation and admiration. Countless thousands of people file past its bullet-proof case in the Louvre, and yet further along the same wall is another picture which, although not so popular, embodies many of the Renaissance ideals in portraiture.

Baldassare Castiglione by Raphael portrays a serene personification of the courtier as a gentleman. Castiglione was the author of *The Courtier*, a book that describes codes of behaviour for the Renaissance man. It enjoyed vast success, not only in Italy but throughout other parts of Europe and Raphael provides a visual equivalent in the serene countenance of the portrait. The calm and dignified expression coupled with the eloquent yet restrained paint quality sets the precedent for centuries of single figure portraits.

Although Raphael and Leonardo differed as

personalities, they were linked by a conception of the world that was quite different from the northern European view. The achievement of Albrecht Dürer (1471 - 1528) seems more deliberate and less fluent in comparison with Leonardo's work, and it is hard to think of the two artists as contemporaries. Dürer admired the Italians, but he felt that the secrets of their painting eluded him and in 1505 he went to Italy in the hope of discovering them for himself. Despite this pilgrimage and subsequent familiarity with work by Bellini and Leonardo, there exists in his work a conflict between the rational order of Italian Humanism and the disjointed, traditional aspects of the Gothic world. The paintings of Raphael and Leonardo exude technical confidence as well as a general sense of assurance between man and the world. The haunting presence of some of Dürer's images, his *Self-portrait* for example, although in step with technical innovation, presents a vulnerable and uncertain image of man.

This kind of conflict is not so apparent in the work of another German painter, the younger

FAR LEFT Detail of **Ginevra de' Benci**, Leonardo da Vinci. This portrait is generally considered to be of Ginevra de' Benci, painted between 1474 and 1478 to celebrate the occasion of her marriage, although there has been some doubt. The theory is, however, supported by the existence of a prickly juniper tree in the background, framing the subject's face; **ginevra** or **ginepro** means 'juniper' in Italian. This type of visual pun on names was common during the Renaissance and Leonardo made full use of it here, with the lady's pale skin looking almost translucent in front of the semi-opaque glazes of the evergreen.

LEFT **Mona Lisa**, Leonardo da Vinci. The model for this timeless portrait was Lisa Gheradini, the wife of Francesco di Zanobi del Giocondo. The enigmatic smile of the Gioconda has been spoken and written about since the painting was first displayed, and it is interesting that the way she seems to smile with only the left part of her mouth accords with a piece of advice given to Renaissance women by Agnolo Firenzuola in a book on beauty and etiquette. He suggested: 'From time to time, to close the mouth at the right corner with a suave and nimble movement, and to open it at the left side, as if you were smiling secretly...this is not affectation, if it is done in a restrained and graceful manner and accompanied by innocent coquetry and by certain movements of the eyes...' Whether the **Mona Lisa** influenced this ideal or was influenced by it, it is certain that the picture, so different from others of the time, constitutes a landmark in the development of portraiture. The seated pose is relaxed, almost informal, and the mood of the subject enhanced by the mysterious landscape and sombre colouring.

Hans Holbein (1497 - 1543), who was more cosmopolitan than Dürer and, through his travels, was able to reap the full benefits of Renaissance painting while maintaining his own individuality. During the disturbances of the Reformation, Holbein visited England, where he painted a remarkable portrait of Henry VIII.

Renaissance concepts found fruition in Holbein's vision of the world, and his depiction of philosophers and scholars as well as merchants and the aristocracy shows how he had developed despite the religious and artistic conflicts which occurred after the Reformation in the sixteenth century. The paintings of Dürer, Lucas Cranach (1472 - 1553) and Mathias Grünewald (c 1460 -1528) include intensely personal characteristics that have since been thought to epitomize Germanic art. The restrained and detached vision of Holbein is less strictly Germanic traits, and yet in the intimate portrait of his wife and children there is an almost cruel awareness of human imperfection that is suppressed in his more impassive descriptions of the aristocracy. In the allegorical portrait of Jean de Dinteville and Georges de Selve known as *The Ambassadors*, Holbein displays a virtuoso performance that typifies his ability to combine a commanding human presence with the attributes of status and success, and a visual acknowledgement of the intellectual and scientific progress of his day. The celebration of earthly success is amended by the introduction of a visual 'memento mori' in the form of the distorted reflection of a skull in the mirror.

During the Renaissance in Italy, various developments took place in different regions and it was in Venice that the exploration of oil paint's potential found its outlet. As a rich and independent city it was open to distant commerce and the people were quick to exploit the commercial possibilities of such an advance. The arts flourished and the demand for pictures was so large that artistic factories developed out of what had been small family concerns. Giovanni Bellini was the most important influence on painters of his own and next generations. Jacopo Bellini (c 1400 - 1470), his father, was also a painter, as were his brother Gentile (c 1429 - 1507) and brother-in-law Andrea Mantegna (1421 - 1506); between them they produced hundreds of religious compositions and portraits.

Bellini was one of the first Italian artists to use oil paint as a medium in itself and quickly realized its potential, the results of which challenged the cool, dry Florentine style. Bellini's vision accommodated a tactile response to the visual world similar to that of the Flemish, yet at the same time a pictorial organization worthy of the best fifteenth-century Italians. One of his most striking portraits is *Doge Leonardo Loredano*. This elderly man swathed in robes has the monumental grandeur and solemnity of a marble statue. Despite the delicate quality of the skin, the bone structure is realized with authority; this is accentuated by the satin robe and intensely blue background.

Bellini's paint application is sober and restrained, yet painters ever since have tried in vain to understand how the richness evolved. This achievement was remarkable considering the exploratory nature of what was then a relatively new medium. The passage of time has only added to the elusiveness of an explanation, the only certainty being that the application of transparent glazes of paint results in a translucent quality that cannot be equalled by the application of opaque paint. His paintings paved the way for the sumptuous paint qualities in the work of Titian (c 1487 - 1576) and Giorgione (1475 - 1510). At the same time, the clarity of Mantegna gave way to a softer more organic feeling in which the effect of light on skin and drapery reached unknown heights.

The confidence with which Bellini's successors Titian and Giorgione painted skin resulted not only in realistic portraiture but extended to reveal the whole figure. The authority with which they dealt with the nude was unprecedented and unequalled in Europe. The frank sensuality, the opulent draperies and luscious landscapes were truly Venetian and quite opposed in spirit to the more overtly intellectual achievement in the rest of Italy. Despite similarities in Giorgione's work and Titian's early pictures, their contrasting temperaments eventually emerged. The graceful subtlety of Giorgione is matched by the vigorous and dramatic aspects of Titian. The official portraits by Titian, including those of his patron Charles V and of Pope Paul II with his grandsons, have interested many portrait painters since, but the lasting effect of his work is due to the influence of the less formal portraits that with relaxed yet animated postures are remarkably modern in concept.

With few exceptions the artists of the sixteenth century were seemingly intimidated by the formidable artistic achievements made in the High Renaissance. It was not until the twentieth century that a recognizable difference between the Renaissance and the Baroque era was acknowledged. Michelangelo Buonarroti (1475 - 1564), who outlived both Raphael and Leonardo by more than 40 years, had a considerable influence on the next generations of Italian painters. His sculptural devotion to the male nude provided the inspiration for the frenzied schemes of wilfully distorted groups of figures that are usually termed Mannerist and find their most overt realization in the work of Jacopo Pontormo (1494 -1557) and Parmigianino

LEFT **Portrait of Erasmus** (1523), Hans Holbein. A powerful study in character, this portrait shows the humanist scholar at work in his study, his profile clearly etched against a curtain. Erasmus moved to Basel in 1521 where Holbein lived and worked; this picture was painted during the struggles for the Reformation. When the Reformation brought a decline in patronage, Erasmus gave Holbein an introduction to Sir Thomas More in England, where the artist went to look for commissions.

RIGHT **Self-portrait**, Albrecht Dürer. Using pen and ink on paper, Dürer drew this self-portrait at the age of 22, having already developed an individual style. His use of hatching and crosshatching illustrate an assured grasp of form and volume, also visible in the hand and pillow sketches. The confident lines of the portrait display enquiring eyes and a slight, humoured scepticism.

ABOVE **The Ambassadors,** Hans Holbein. This famous double portrait was commissioned in 1533 and displays great detail and imaginative use of oil colors. The objects ranged on the chest probably referred to the particular interests of the two men and emphasize Renaissance learning.

RIGHT **Baldassare Castiglione,** Raphael. The piercing blue eyes of Count Castiglione confront the spectator with a demanding honesty, while his benignity probably expresses the view of the man who was held by his peers to be an authority on etiquette. Raphael's fluid paint techniques suit the mood of contentment.

(1503 - 40). The sober vision of Bronzino (1503 -72), a pupil of Pontormo, reveals a remarkable penetration in the field of portraiture. The restrained colour, which is untypical of Mannerist painting, emphasizes the icy grandeur of his aristocratic subjects, who in alert postures and with expressions of disdain, confront the world with an inscrutability that anticipates the portraits of Ingres (1780 - 1867). In Bronzino's portraits of children there is a more immediate human involvement yet even here an element of unease behind the immaculate paint surface. In the portrait of Giovanni de Medici (1475), the young boy's gleeful expression is matched by the way he grasps the bird in a chubby hand. Within the limitations of what at first appear to be straightforward half-length portraits, Bronzino achieves subtlety as well as variety. The positioning of the hands is always crucial to the design of the painting and invariably draws attention to the pictorial accessories, competing with the head as an immediate focal point.

Bronzino's strength as a portrait painter is partly due to an ability to reconcile human imperfection with an abstract purity of design. In *Portrait of a Young Man* (c 1529) the sense of pictorial harmony might suggest a somewhat idealized vision of what has been considered a self-portrait. On closer inspection, the cleanshaven purity of the head belies a frank acknowledgement of imperfection in the divergent squint of the left eye. At the bottom edge of the painting, the gargoyle-like caricatures decorating the arm of the chair and the stone ledge contrast violently with the calm superiority of the portrait. It has been suggested that the sophistication of Mannerist imagery implied a similar sophistication on the part of the viewer. However, it was a violent rejection of this acquired attitude that marked the subtle vision of Caravaggio (1573 - 1610).

Few painters since Giotto have had such a fundamental impact on the course of Western painting as Caravaggio. The idea of the artist as a rebel is common to the twentieth century but at the end of a century that had paid homage to the achievements made during the Renaissance, it was an anathema. Caravaggio's early death added potency to a notorious reputation that had encompassed a personal and artistic confrontation with the established opinions. His career was violently criticized and there was controversy surrounding his religious works which were often rejected on the grounds of indecorum. However, his paintings were appreciated by astute collectors. The main reason for the conflict surrounding his work is not easily discernible in retrospect, but his delight in presenting solemn religious themes with a frank reality challenged the very foundations of pictorial convention in the sixteenth century. His intolerance of the repetition of forms in the style of Michelangelo and Raphael forced him to strike out alone and resulted in remarkable work, based on observation and not the precedents set by others. The main objection to Caravaggio's art resulted from his blatant acknowledgement of visual phenomena and an unwillingness to present the spiritual world in anything not visually tangible.

As modern x-ray evidence has shown, Caravaggio's painting method involved compositional changes being made while working; this would substantiate the argument that he did not rely on preparational studies and drawings. It also suggests that he worked directly from models, and by so doing he produced images with individual rather than preconceived characteristics. In this respect, Caravaggio's religious subjects can be interpreted as groups of portraits of people acting out religious roles. The theatrical metaphor is also appropriate considering that the space his figures occupy invariably takes the form of an enclosed box which eliminates the necessity of indicating landscape, the main province of previous Italian painting. He was fond of painting figures in contemporary dress and juxtaposing these quite blatantly with figures in robes that are often associated with allegorical or religious subjects. The sense of drama that pervades Caravaggio's work is enhanced by the implications of a powerful light source emphasizing the volumes of figures depicted; this does not attempt to convey the kind of spirituality apparent in the work of El Greco (1541 - 1614) or Tintoretto (1518 - 94).

Caravaggio's *Conversion of St Paul* records the miraculous event with unprecendented honesty. *The Supper at Emmaus* displays a similar candour in the individual characterization of the figures, except for a slight concession to an idealized Christ figure. The man on the right, seen in profile, is anything but idealized, and it was this emphasis on human imperfection

LEFT **Cardinal Don Fernando Nino de Guevara**, El Greco. Born in Crete, El Greco's real name was Domenikos Theotocopoulos, but he did not stay in his native country. Instead he studied painting in Venice, where the work of Tintoretto and Michelangelo had a great influence, and later in Rome before going on to work in Spain. He was a sculptor as well as a fine painter, mainly concentrating on religious subjects. His unusual style can be seen in this portrait of the Cardinal. El Greco often used bold lighting and the typically large, visible brushstrokes contribute to a feeling of liveliness. He manipulated the brush to create the different textures of silk and lace with great effect. At the same time, the stern aspect of the Cardinal and the way in which he looks down at the spectator create an impression of authority.

RIGHT **Portrait of a Young Man**, Agnolo di Cosimo di Mariano Bronzino. The adopted son and pupil of Pontormo, Bronzino displays the Mannerist penchant for excellent and potentially vigorous physiques and exaggerated poses in this portrait, which has been thought to be of himself. The figure displays an aristocratic disdain and coolness, which is enhanced by the green hue of the plain unwelcoming background.

ABOVE Detail of **The Supper at Emmaus**, Michelangelo Merisi da Caravaggio. The shadowy light of this imagined scene afforded Caravaggio an opportunity to exploit **chiaroscuro** techniques; using these the old man's profile has been most realistically represented. The stretching position of his arms adds enormous vitality and tension to his pose.

RIGHT Detail of **The Topers**, Diego Velasquez. These cheery, drunken faces were painted from live models, probably people from the streets of Madrid, where Velasquez was working as court painter to Philip IV of Spain. Their expressions are utterly believable; apart from the style of dress, the men could easily be imagined on any city street today.

that confounded the expectations of his patrons. In most previous paintings, the sanctity of a religious personage was fully endorsed by a clean exterior that radiated an inner light. By comparison, Caravaggio's saints emerge as ordinary people straight from the streets of Rome or Naples complete with ragged clothes and dirty feet. Often they are projected in ungainly and contorted postures, providing an immediate, seemingly physical confrontation with the viewer that contemporary critics found objectionable.

Caravaggio's influence over artists extended well beyond previous geographical limitations. Although his revolutionary realism inspired imitators closer to home, his true legacy found fruition in the work of Diego Velasquez and Rembrandt van Rijn, and was to be resurrected in the nineteenth century by Gustave Courbet (1819 -77) and the Realist movement.

In comparison with the turbulent life of Caravaggio, that of Velasquez, the Spaniard, was sedate. His confident artistic achievement as a court painter parallels that of his contemporary and friend, Sir Peter Paul Rubens (1577 -1640). Both painters enjoyed early and lasting success at the courts of their respective patrons and yet their opposite temperaments resulted in a completely different artistic development. The grand schemes and painterly flourish of Rubens epitomize the Baroque tendency in painting, of which he is the most important northern exponent, and the sober vision of Velasquez emerges through the confrontation with a single figure and as such occupies a central position in the development of Western portraiture.

The influence of Caravaggio on Velasquez is apparent in many ways. His early work reveals a spontaneous naturalism, and he underplayed any overt expression in an attempt to convey the effect of light on tactile surfaces, using *chiaroscuro*. In the picture known as *The Topers* (*c* 1629), the mythological figures form a theatrical tableau and occupy the bulk of the pictorial space. Landscape exists as a backdrop to the human activity, but the lighting evokes an interior rather than exterior space. Although the three figures at the left of the picture could have emerged from one of many timeless evocations of this subject, the group at the right have a more earthy realism that may have been the result of painting from live models. They reveal a confrontation with the artist or viewer, and probably represent quite accurate, informal portraits, although their identities are unknown.

A tension exists between the specific description of an individual model and the character that the model depicts. In other words, the figures in *The Topers* owe their credibility not to the fact that they are taking part in some mythological story or pagan rite but to the degree in which they are acting out their roles in a dramatic reconstruction. The figures are believable because they were probably posed in a studio and their individual characteristics acknowledged rather than underplayed.

Considering the ability with which Velasquez was able to characterize groups of figures, it is not surprising that when he was confronted by just one, he was able to convey a great intensity. As Velasquez matured, his technique became more sophisticated and the economic handling of paint enabled him to convey a solidity of form with atmospheric depth. Unlike Rubens, he had no need to display his virtuosity as a painter; instead, his disciplined vision evolved through an increasing subtlety. This is evident in the remarkable portrait of Pope Innocent X.

Previous pontiffs had been immortalized but Velasquez' work is different because it portrays the man inside the public image. Similarly, his portraits of Philip IV reveal an unsure man cloaked in the trappings of power, the grandeur of which belies a sense of innocence and vulnerability. By contrast, the portrait of Don Diego de Acedo, who was known as 'El Primo', is presented with the attributes of adminstrative status. Although the physical burden accentuates the subject's tiny body, the facial expression reveals a thoughtful man whose burden is in fact the society that finds his disability a source of amusement. Portraits by Velasquez do not celebrate human imperfection; instead they acknowledge human individuality with compassion and understanding, and as such can be ranked among the highest achievements in European portraiture.

The culmination of Velasquez' work is a large group portrait entitled *Las Meninas (The Maids of Honour)*. The almost effortless depiction of reality evident in the compact compositional structure gives way to a paradoxical interpretation that questions the fundamental nature of illusion. The self-portrait at the left of the picture implies that the picture could have been the view seen by Velasquez himself in a large mirror. If this logic is continued, then it could also be assumed that the reflection of the royal couple in a mirror behind Velasquez would imply their

real position in front of and facing the main group of figures. If this were the case, the royal couple would also be visible with their backs reflected into the mirror that Velasquez would have used in order to paint the group in such a way. To further complicate any logical interpretation, he painted himself working on a large support that could be understood as the back of the completed painting in question. The visual paradox involved in this picture defies any rational explanation but it suggests a concern by the painter to stress the difference between the structure of a painting as a separate entity, and the deception caused by an acceptance of what purports to be real.

The careers of Velasquez and Rembrandt are interestingly contrasted. Both painters emerged from the influence of Caravaggio, and both display a constant preoccupation with portraiture, and yet the secluded, ordered world of the Spanish court could not be further removed from the conflicting political and religious concerns evident in the small Dutch nation. The Dutch won their independence from Spain by a 40-year truce in 1609 and then produced some of the most influential painters that Western culture has known. Unlike the aristocratic monarchies of England, France and Spain, social status was measured by acquired wealth and not hereditary circumstances. The art reflected the taste of the Protestant middle class

and found fruition in the depiction of day-to-day life. Contemporary records substantiate the fact that pictures were bought by people from different social levels, and although there was little patronage for religious works, the domestic interior, the still life and the figure became the secular vehicles for both moral and religious concerns. The sumptuous still life paintings of Willem Heda (1593/4 - 1680/2) make reference to the vanity of earthly gratifications, Rembrandt's biblical themes emerge in domestic settings, and the pristine interiors of Vermeer (1632 - 75) reveal ideas that transcend the apparent concern with domesticity.

In Utrecht, the widespread interest in the work of Caravaggio emerged through the paintings of Hendrick Terbrugghen (1588 - 1629). One of his favourite images was the single figure *genre* subject that usually took the form of a solitary musician or singer isolated against a simple background. Even in his religious compositions Terbrugghen depicted the biblical personages with a down-to-earth realism, often stressing the irregularity of their features and making no concessions to the many idealized images of the past.

In Haarlem, Frans Hals (1581/5 - 1666) became the chief exponent of portraiture. The popularity of his paintings is partly due to the depiction of optimism and gaiety. The early paintings, particularly, convey with vitality

LEFT **Regents of the Old Men's Home**, Frans Hals. Painted only two years before his death, this group portrait of the female regents is typical of Hals' later style. The composition is simple but strong, and the monochromatic tones do not detract from the interest of the picture. Each face portrays great character; despite their individuality, however, the women seem united and contented in their shared vocation.
RIGHT **Hendrijke Stoffels**, Rembrandt van Rijn. This portrait is of Rembrandt's devoted mistress who lived with him until she died in 1663. Her expression seems full of tenderness; similarly her image is painted with an unmistakable depth of feeling. The portrait is imbued with harmony, not only in the emotions portrayed but in the simplicity of composition, the relaxed and contented pose and the soft lighting which enhances the texture of her jacket and the gentleness of her face.

expressions of laughter and happiness, and although they were often contained within a traditional format there is a liveliness that is seldom equalled by his contemporaries. As his reputation grew, he was able to secure important commissions that provided a rare opportunity in seventeenth-century Holland to paint large works for public display. They included six life-size portraits of militia groups, three group portraits of Regents, and four family groups. The two group portraits painted two years before his death are generally considered his most powerful works. They depict the male and female Regents of the Old Men's Home, and the economic paint handling combines solidity with strikingly individual portraits. Each head forms a focal point within the group and yet both paintings are unified by compositional strength and a simple tonal structure.

Although Hals was employed as a portrait painter for most of his life, other painterly styles became more fashionable during the seventeenth century. Rembrandt van Rijn is the name that remains synonymous with the golden age of Dutch painting. In terms of insight into human experience, Rembrandt has been universally acclaimed and seldom surpassed. However, there was always a conflict in his mind between the need to produce commissioned portraits and the desire to paint for personal reasons. Eventually the private obsession dominated, but earlier in his career he was able to satisfy the demands of his patrons with prodigious and innovative results.

Rembrandt's qualities as a portrait painter were apparent from the beginning of his career, and his early explorations in self-portraiture reveal a man whose original vision would not be

suppressed by the outmoded conventions of many of his contemporaries. The beginning of his success unfolds with the innovatory handling of *The Anatomy Lesson of Dr Tulp*. The picture, compared with previous attempts at the same subject, is quite revolutionary in concept and was received enthusiastically. In seventeenth-century Holland the dissection of a corpse for anatomical study was a common event, and the popularity of such displays often resulted in the admission of the public with audiences of up to 300 people. The problem of combining a group of figures in such a way that each was recognizable yet contributed to a common activity, had resulted in artificial groupings in previous Dutch attempts. However, Rembrandt chose to depict a private group in which Dr Tulp is performing surgery for the benefit of a group

of students in natural poses, positioned so that, despite a similarity of dress, there is variety in posture. The simple white ruffs worn by the men become a strong compositonal element and not just an excuse for repetition. The figure straining forward to see the corpse is an innovative introduction, providing a sense of animation that contrasts with the solidity of the surrounding figures.

Rembrandt made use of a similar device 30 years later in *The Board of the Clothmakers' Guild*, a group portrait of five corporation officials engaged in examining accounts. Once again the severity of the design is relieved by one of the figures who appears to be midway between sitting and standing. With the help of photography, the twentieth century is familiar with figures caught or frozen while moving, but

RIGHT **Girl with a Pearl Earring**, Jan Vermeer. It seems extraordinary that even towards the end of the last century Vermeer's pictures were hardly known; this portrait was bought in the early 1880s at a sale in The Hague for the sum of five shillings. It is a touching work and takes a closer view of its subject than Vermeer's **genre** pictures which usually show the women involved in some kind of occupation, for example reading, needlework, carrying water or playing the virginals. This portrait is unusual because the girl is placed ambiguously against a darkened background, and has no specific pursuit. The only reference to her time is her clothing. However, although unnamed, the portrait was without doubt painted using a live model. Vermeer succeeded in capturing in solid form the mood of a moment.

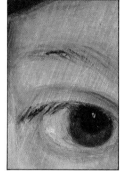

LEFT **Susanna Lunden**, Sir Peter Paul Rubens. In opposition to his contemporary Nicolas Poussin, who believed in the absolute importance of design in painting, Rubens advocated the vitality of colour, and his attitude is evident in this portrait. Susanna, later to become Rubens' sister-in-law, is depicted in splendid, sensuous reds and greens. The materials of her dress are as rich in texture as they are warm in tone. The luxurious plumage of her hat is matched by the heavy billowing clouds behind her. The focal point of the painting is her full bosom. Rubens has painted the flesh tones in layers of overlaid colour, and the white highlights are almost opaque. The pinks and reds are offset by their complementary greens and the whole effect is lightened by the indigo blue sky. ABOVE Rubens' techniques are visible in this detail of Susanna's right eye. The streaked greyish underpainting gives depth to the shadows under thin glazes, while pink and white paint highlight the forms of her nose and eye.

in the seventeenth century, this novel approach ensured Rembrandt's reputation for originality. In both instances Rembrandt was able to comply with his clients' wishes while at the same time pursuing his own interests and inclinations. His own knowledge, and an awareness of Italian art, contributed considerably to the development of a personal vision that was considered unique even by his contemporaries.

As Rembrandt gained more independence as a painter, his attitude to his work changed and the youthful exuberance gave way to introspection, brought about by the tragedy of his wife's death a year after giving birth to their only surviving son. As van Dyck's paintings became more fashionable with the wealthy art circles in Amsterdam, Rembrandt's work became less popular. He abandoned many of his social contracts, consequently got into debt and turned inward in an attempt to alleviate his misery. Props were discarded in favour of simplicity. The single figure shrouded in darkness became the vehicle for his interest, and light, not on the face but within it, the central unifying force.

A pupil of Rembrandt and probably the teacher of Vermeer, Carel Fabritius (1622 - 54) encompasses the *chiaroscuro* of the former with a foretaste of the high-key palette of the latter in his work. With few exceptions, Rembrandt's pictures involve an illuminated figure set against a dark background; in Vermeer's pictures, the reverse is true with the exception of early work and one or two tiny portrait heads. Most of his figures occupy a defined space and are positioned against a brilliantly illuminated wall surface. In his self-portrait, the bold *chiaroscuro* of Rembrandt is combined with a background wall surface that is light in tone.

Vermeer's work is full of paradox. Although he is not considered a portrait painter in the accepted sense, his images of women in domestic interiors have a credibility that suggests the artist made studies of particular individuals. The fact that Vermeer often favoured the use of profile is also surprising considering his apparent interest in optics and the degree to which the profile is usually associated with artifice. Perhaps the most disconcerting aspects of his output are the apparent lack of transition from early to later work, and his immaculate painting technique and smooth surfaces that accentuate the implied emotional distance between subject and artist or spectator. In many cases he emphasized the gap with furniture, curtains or an empty space in the foreground.

Vermeer's most famous single figure portrait is the *Girl with a Pearl Earring*, whose enigmatic presence has been compared with that of the *Mona Lisa*. The beautiful quality of understatement found in the simple oval head is echoed by the shape of the earring. As may be noticed in the almost imperceptible tonal transition from the nose to the light side of the cheek, Vermeer disregards the more generally accepted ways of

describing volume. Similar examples of this technique occur throughout his work and suggest an awareness of the way in which the optical anomalies found in nature differ from the painterly devices used to imply solidity. Since the early Renaissance the solidity of a head had usually been described by a single light that emphasized volume in a pronounced way. If the girl's head in Vermeer's portrait had been lit from the righthand side, the nose would have cast a shadow on the portion of the face furthest from the spectator, and the volume of the head would have been evident in the conventional way. Vermeer, however, seems deliberately to have shunned such practice and yet achieves a sense of volume in an infinitely more subtle way. The way the girl is caught in the movement of glancing over her shoulder becomes timeless in his hands.

The political decline of the Italian states and the rising nationalism of both Protestant and Catholic countries in the seventeenth century resulted in Holland, Spain and Flanders nurturing artistic proficiency in a way that had previously only been encouraged within the religious orbit of the papacy. The careers of two artists of differing temperaments can be seen to represent the opposite poles of artistic concern

at this time. The respective contributions of Sir Peter Paul Rubens and Nicolas Poussin (1593/4 - 1665) provided the springboard for a conflict that has occurred in varying guises ever since. Poussin is remembered essentially for his depictions of classical and mythological subjects rendered with an obsessive emphasis on geometric structure and organization. Although he did paint portraits, and had a considerable influence on Western painting, he was more concerned to represent idealized human images. Philosophically his attitude represented the antithesis of Rubens' turbulent world.

With the election to the Academy of Rubens' biographer, the course of French painting in the eighteenth century was decided. Although classical subjects were preserved, they were deprived of their intellectual rigour and a frivolity and self-indulgence in paintings of the human form emerged. Francois Boucher (1703 - 70) was one of the chief exponents of female nude painting, the object of which can only be regarded as lascivious, and with the exception of a few striking pictures his *oeuvre* is characterized by a lack of regard for individuality, and a concern for the trivial. Jean-Baptiste Chardin (1699 - 1779) stands apart from the prevailing concerns of this style and has more in common with the example

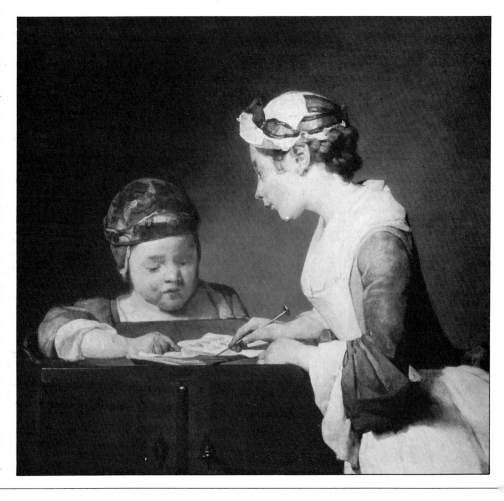

FAR LEFT **The Young Schoolmistress**, Jean-Baptiste Siméon Chardin. Running parallel to the fashionable Rococo style in eighteenth-century France was a simple naturalism similar to the Dutch **genre** pictures painted the century before. This picture is an example of Chardin's direct portrayal of everyday life.
LEFT **Self-portrait**, Carel Fabritius. It is probable that this is a portrait of the artist himself. Fabritius was a pupil of Rembrandt, and learnt to use limited colours combined with subtle tonal contrasts for effective results.

BELOW **The Death of Marat**, Jacques-Louis David. Marat was a martyr to the cause of the Revolution, and David, a fervent supporter of Napoleon Bonaparte, painted this emotive death portrait in an attempt to raise the event to the level of universal tragedy. Later, he considered it one of his best paintings. The work is unusual in that half of it is quite empty, and the room, cast in a green shadow, echoes with its dreadful secret. The dramatic position of the arms draws attention to the lolling head and the unfinished missive.

set in Holland during the previous century. His figures are generally incorporated into domestic interiors and with few exceptions they are depicted as though unaware of the artist's presence.

Except for isolated examples, painting in the eighteenth century cannot compete with the contemporary literary and musical achievements, and the course of French painting in particular could not be further removed from the era of Rationalism which it parallels. Portraits continued to be painted although in most cases as a document of social standing. In England, however, portraiture emerged independently and, for the first time, did not rely on foreign influence. The achievements of Holbein, Lely (1618 - 80) and van Dyck (1599 - 1614) had previously been considered awesome, but by the eighteenth century the English could boast of native talent in the work of Sir Joshua Reynolds

(1723 - 92), William Hogarth (1697 - 1764) and Thomas Gainsborough (1727 - 88). The contributions of these three were very individual. Reynolds was influenced by the high ideals of the Renaissance and ignored Dutch realism, as he was convinced that art should be respected as a form of ethical education. Hogarth, on the other hand, was determined to expose the hypocrisy and immorality of society and concentrated on the portrayal of affectation and abuse in satirical pictures. The incisive and spontaneous qualities of his work are obvious in his sympathetic sketch, *A Shrimp Girl*. Gainsborough's portraits are painted in a distinctive, elegant style that reflects the preoccupations of the gentry and aristocracy in the eighteenth century.

Bartolomé Murillo (1617 - 82) lived in seventeenth-century Seville. Apart from his many fine religious and allegorical paintings, his portraits of children stand out with an unusual

freshness. His pictures of street urchins are notably vivid, and he could be considered to have invented child portraiture. However, probably the most significant personality to emerge in Spain was Francisco de Lucientes Goya (1746 -1828). Although in France the excesses of the Baroque and Rococo eras were tempered by a return to sobriety in the form of neo-Classicism, no other single artist could compare with Goya. Like so many painters, he defies categorization. Despite his early sojourn into fashionable frivolity, his portraits of the Spanish royal family display an intense realism. In other later portraits, it is obvious that he had studied the effects of poses and expressions, and his strong individual vision revealed itself in a confident use of contrasting lights. He emerges as a painter who with prophetic insight anticipated the trauma of events of which the rest of Europe seemed unaware.

The storming of the Bastille in 1789 heralded a new era. Paris emerged as the centre of a political and artistic revolution of international significance. The Revolution and Napoleon's rise to supreme power was celebrated by Jacques Louis David (1748 - 1825) whose passionate political involvement resulted in a series of paintings praising both classical and Republican virtues. The enormous *Coronation of Napoleon* involves over 100 portraits and demonstrates the degree to which David's fanaticism was apparent. A more modest yet probably more memorable piece of propaganda is evident in *The Death of Marat*, a powerful portrait of one of the Revolution's martyrs, depicted with the dramatic intensity usually reserved for religious personages. Baroque elegance is replaced by an uncompromising severity that epitomizes the neo-Classical concern with drawing. Marat's bath has been rightly compared to a tomb, and the use of a large empty space above the figure accentuates its stark simplicity.

The disciplined vision of David inspired many imitators in the classical tradition. The apex of this pictorial ideology also provided the basis of a rebellion against the vigorous classical principles and became the Romantic movement. Although, paradoxically, both attitudes shared a dissatisfaction with government and culture,

ABOVE LEFT **Nelly O'Brien**, Sir Joshua Reynolds. The first President of the Royal Academy, Reynolds was the most important and influential British artist of his day. Having travelled through Europe and studied the works of Italian Renaissance artists, he returned to London determined to educate young artists in the classical ideal, urging them to study the works of Michelangelo and Raphael. Portraiture, he held, should be considered in the grand manner, because the beauty of art consists in rising above 'singular forms, local customs, particularities, and details of every kind'. In consequence, some portraits by Reynolds take on a rigidity of form and a detachment which belies his sensitivity. By contrast, this portrait, painted in 1763, indicates a vital interest in the individual and an acute response to the subject. The mood is comfortable and

displays an intimacy between artist and subject. Nelly O'Brien is seated in a richly coloured woodland scene; the paints have been used to render dappled light and the textures of the clothing with great subtlety. Her blue eyes confront the spectator with a gentle honesty.

ABOVE RIGHT **The Shrimp Girl**, William Hogarth. The individuality and precision of Hogarth's art lies in his acute awareness of the injustice and immorality buried within society. To bring these absurdities to the public eye, he satirized anecdotes in sequences of pictures both painted and engraved; famous examples are **A Rake's Progress** and **Marriage à la Mode.** When painting portraits he proved incapable of affectation and flattery, but was confident and displayed enormous common sense. **The Shrimp Girl** is a delightfully lively portrait, although a simple sketch. The colours are thin

and the brushstrokes brief, except for the face which is illuminated in flushed pinks and highlights. Her expression could not be described as sophisticated; she illustrates the innocence and courage of a girl likely to take advantage of whatever life offers.

RIGHT **Monsieur Bertin**, Jean Auguste Dominique Ingres. The portrait is positioned within the shape of the canvas so that the picture is weighted in the lower half; this, combined with the precise delineation of the shape of the body, illustrates Ingres' concern with composition and the way it influences the mood of a portrait. The almost sculptured solidity of the figure is emphasized by the triangular surface structure combined with the sombre colours, the greying hair and dark clothing. It is all painted in minute detail and with great realism. Bertin's hands are fleshy but firm; these

and his face are the lightest and therefore most immediately noticed elements of the painting. The hands, however, are not relaxed but are flexed, as if he is almost resting his weight, but is in reality on the verge of moving. This aspect, combined with the expression of his face which is kind in its severity and seems about to betray some emotion, gives a strong impression of impending movement. This creates a tension with the superficial sturdiness of the picture.

ABOVE **The Burial at Ornans**, Gustave Courbet. The artist was 31 when this picture was exhibited at the Paris Salon of 1850, attracting both the attention and the dismay of onlookers. The life-size display of the ordinary existence of ordinary people shocked the Romanticists and Classicists alike, because Courbet had removed the veils of illusion. Courbet said: 'Painting is an art of sight and should therefore concern itself with things seen'. The group portrait, including members of his family and some of his friends, is vividly drawn, with every character involved in some action. The gaping grave in the foreground unites the opposing groups of the churchmen and the mourners in an awareness of a common fate.
RIGHT Detail of **The Bellelli**

Family, Edgar Degas. In this portrait of Degas' aunt and her family, the artist has created a compositional structure that reveals the tensions known to exist within the family. Degas could not have failed to notice the problems during his nine-month stay with them in 1858 and 1859. The gloomy and impatient Baron is painted in shadow and slightly out of focus. His unusual position with his back to the spectator is contrasted with his wife's sorrowful but upright stance. The sympathetic lighting bathing the daughters and the mother creates a unity between them which conflicts with the hunched and darkened form of the father. An emotional complexity is thus defined within the rectangle of the canvas.

they provided the focal points of almost irreconcilable tendencies in painting. Prior to its effect on French painting, Romanticism had emerged in a literary form in England and Germany, and invariably conjured up a mood of fanciful escapism suggested by desolate ruins, murky forests and atmospheric landscapes. Although painters of both persuasions evolved a pictorial language that was specifically representational, the underlying concerns were quite different philosophically. Jean Auguste Dominique Ingres proved to be David's most original pupil and is generally accepted to be an important exponent of classical ideas, while his rival Eugène Delacroix (1798 - 1863) provided a formidable argument in favour of Romanticism. From a technical point of view the classical preference for linear structure opposes the more overtly emotional and expressive use of colour in Romantic painting. However, this generalization cannot accommodate the anomalies that occur in the work of individual exponents.

The Romantic generation responded to the banality of everyday existence by travelling abroad, and much of the material used by

Delacroix was the result of his exotic journey to Morocco in 1832. The complex allegorical and historical subjects of his paintings provided a form of political escapism and were intended to be, in his own words, 'a feast for the eyes'. His portraits included some intimate and revealing studies of friends, for example Chopin (1838), but his more expressive and exuberant nature enabled him to excel in large and complex compositions.

By comparison, Ingres provided an intellectual journey back through time in an attempt to recreate a view of antiquity through nineteenth-century eyes. The slow research and obsessive consideration for preparatory study hindered Ingres in his ambition to be a great history painter, and although he considered portraiture to be a less worthy occupation it proved to be his greatest achievement. It could be argued that his portraits present the last significant examples of traditional Western portraits that acknowledge a social order behind the subject, but, at the same time, their fascination lies in the diversity of individual appearance trapped within a relatively orthodox format. Despite the fact that Ingres had neither the imagination nor the pictorial invention of Delacroix, his paintings present an authority which was the product of acute observation and an ability to transform his perception into something timeless. His male subjects confront the viewer with a relaxed confidence and aloofness, and occasionally, as in the portrait of Monsieur Bertin (1832), with a formidable presence that is accentuated by the imposing sculptural posture. By comparison, his female subjects, Madame de Senonnes for example, emerge as the embodiment of the decaying age of indolence.

Unlike many painters who in later life evolved a more spontaneous technique, Ingres obstinately persisted with his original style in spite of the radical developments being made around him. Few portrait painters since have immortalized their patrons with such skill and uncompromising clarity. However, the re-evaluation of the artist's position within an established order resulted in an increasing gulf between those who paint portraits on a commissioned basis and those who paint portraits for personal reasons. Gustave Courbet emerged at the forefront of the Realist movement in painting, intent on using the language of painting as a truthful reflection of contemporary life. Not only did he challenge the established extremes of Classicism and Romanticism, but he questioned the role of the artist in society to such a degree that the repercussions are still apparent.

By elevating an everyday occurrence to the level of importance usually reserved for a religious or historical subject, Courbet opened the way for an attitude that was to be reflected in literary as well as visual achievements. In *The Burial at Ornans*, exhibited in 1850, he presents a life-size description of the mourners at a funeral,

all linked by the thought of a common fate regardless of their station in life. The figures are portraits of Courbet's friends and family standing in rows at the graveside. The impact of such a picture was unforgettable, and its apparent banality and lack of conventional drama confused many critics who considered it to be an outrageous joke, an irreverent evocation of a solemn event. The political implications of Courbet's visual democracy did not go unnoticed and became the object of ridicule.

Since Courbet, many artists have adopted the role of an outsider in society and have produced work regardless of the endorsement or acknowledgement of that society. Consequently the portrait has become less evident in its traditional role, and as the mainstream of painting has veered further away from the established views, so the portrait has emerged as an informal depiction of an individual rather than a public display of status.

The advent of photography was another reason for the decline of traditional portraiture. Initially photographers sought to imitate the conventions of Western painting, and it was assumed that the new invention would make painting obsolete by providing a more immediate means of fixing human appearance. The experiments of Nicéphore Niépce (1765 -1833) and Louis Daguerre (1789 - 1851) were successful, but although the French were quick to realize the potential of photography, other nations remained sceptical. An account from the *Leipzig City Advertiser* reveals how threatening the invention appeared to people in the nineteenth century: 'To try to catch transient reflected images is not merely something that is impossible, but as thorough German investigation has shown, the very desire to do so is blasphemy. Man is created in the image of God, and God's image cannot be captured by an human machine. Only the divine artist, divinely inspired, may call on his genius to dare to reproduce the divine human features, but never by means of a mechanical aid.'

Such wishful thinking may have reassured the flagging spirits of aspiring portrait painters, but some serious nineteenth-century artists, including Ingres, Delacroix and Courbet, were quick to exploit photography as an aid. A more significant awareness of its use, however, is to be found in the work of Edouard Manet (1832 - 83) and Edgar Degas (1834 - 1917). Although firmly rooted in their essentially conservative, bourgeois backgrounds and unimpressed by Courbet's socialist views, Manet and Degas were nevertheless affected by his visual authority and the unprecedented realism of his approach.

Normally associated with the Impressionist revolution of the mid-nineteenth century, Manet and Degas are in fact only tenuously linked by a rejection of the prevailing academicism. Ironically, Manet wanted public acceptance, yet his choice of subject provoked bitter criticism,

LEFT **Self-portrait**, Paul Cézanne. From the artist's appearance, this self-portrait is thought to have been painted in about 1880, by which time he had developed an individual set of colour theories and painting techniques. Cézanne carefully considered and monitored the layers of overlaid colour and small, obvious brushstrokes used for large-scale hatching.
Simultaneously, he calculated the juxtaposition of certain hues and tones above, below or beside others for precise effects. Here, reds, yellows, blues, greens, creams and greys are worked into the face, with the final effect of lights and shadows creating a dark and withdrawn portrait.

RIGHT Detail of **Dr Gachet**, Vincent van Gogh. The artist has exploited the descriptive character of his brushstrokes to emphasize the forms of the face, including the nose, cheekbones and eyebrows. The marks of the bristle brush are often apparent in the thick paint and give an actual raised texture to the painting. The lively techniques and van Gogh's particular vision combine to create this intelligent, bright-eyed portrait.

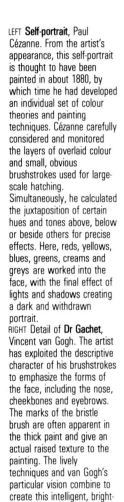

especially through his depiction of the nude figure. The frank realism of the painting entitled *Olympia* (1863) proved too much for contemporary morality, and although its historical precedent existed in the work of Titian and Giorgione, its blatant reliance on the depiction of a nude woman devoid of allegorical or classical attributes resulted in hostility. The fact that the woman acknowledges the presence of a spectator implied that its intention was provocative and therefore challenged the normally accepted canons of pictorial decency.

Degas may be considered the most complex personality of the later part of the nineteenth century, and his connection with the Impressionists is paradoxical. Whereas Courbet openly rejected both Classicism and Romanticism and forged his own path through Realism, Degas at-

tempted to reconcile these tendencies in his own work and always maintained strong respect for his predecessors, unlike many of his contemporaries. Also, during the middle of the nineteenth century there was a rediscovery of seventeenth-century painters and in particular the Dutch *genre* masters. The re-evaluation certainly affected Degas' progress. His involvement with photography and the influence of the simple beauty of imported Japanese art, combined to arm him with sufficient material to shape his own pictorial language. Degas portrayed people as though they were about to move or were in the process of some activity, and consequently revolutionized the concept of portraiture and brought it in step with other contemporary achievements.

Degas' portraits are essentially informal and

intimate, and another aspect of his paradoxical nature emerges in his treatment of *genre* subjects. *The Absinth Drinker* (c 1876) presents what appears to be a slice of contemporary life. However, the depiction of something that was apparently casual became a problem of theatrical deceit, because Degas manufactured a situation by employing professional models or friends to adopt the roles required. As with *The Topers* by Velasquez, the painting purports to be something it is not; posing as a drinking scene, it is presented through the informal portraits of Marcellin Desboutin and Ellen André.

Degas' deliberate portraits were painted with striking originality. An example of this style is the portrait of Viscomte Ludovic Lepic and his daughters, known as *Place de la Concorde*. The apparently normal street scene does not offer

any clues or reasons to explain its use as a setting for the portraits. Combined with this unusual aspect of the painting is the fact that Degas abhorred outdoor painting which he compared to angling. When so many of his contemporaries advocated painting directly in front of the landscape, Degas pursued his experiments indoors regardless of the innovations being made in the depiction of changing light and atmosphere.

Reality is implied in the subtlety of his compositional structure. Although an initial glimpse of *Place de la Concorde* suggests movement, the sense of animation is in fact conveyed by the repetition of similar poses and the tension this causes. The figure of Ludovic is seen as though he is striding across the picture, and his implied movement is accentuated in the position of a similar male figure at the left of the picture. The daughters provide implied movement in the opposite direction by the slight difference in their similar positions; they are dressed in the same way and could at first glance appear to depict the same girl as though seen through different frames of an animated film. The technique of the visual echo is a common occurence in Degas' work, and may be seen frequently in the compositions of ballet dancers. In effect, Degas manages to persuade the spectator that he is witnessing a fleeting glimpse of reality, and yet on closer inspection the illusion is the result of a sophisticated organization of space. Degas positioned the main point of interest at the side in many of his pictures and made use of empty spaces in such a way that they are just as important as the figures.

The need for portraiture emerged with the development of realism in the fifteenth century, and its continuation before this century mostly occurred in situations where that need combined with wealth and patronage. In the twentieth century, the existence of traditional portraiture has been overshadowed by radical departures of intention in art, and there has been a general

decline of interest in figurative depiction. R.B. Kitaj (b 1932) observed in *The Artist's Eye* (1980): 'The period that separates us from 1900, surely one of the most terrible histories of bad faith ever, should somehow conceive and nourish a life of forms increasingly divorced from the illustration of human life which had been art's main province before.'

However, despite the general dissatisfaction with representational art, few major late nineteenth- and early twentieth-century painters have refrained from painting portraits. Vincent van Gogh (1853 - 90) believed portraiture required serious consideration, and Henri Matisse (1869 - 1954) and Pablo Picasso (1881 - 1973), among many others, have used it to express their own visions. It is ironic that Paul Cézanne (1839 - 1906), whose work was inspired by the natural

world of organic forms including the human body, should influence the development of abstract art forms which seem divorced from any kind of external reality. The common aim of naturalistic representation disappeared with the Impressionists in the late nineteenth century, since which time portraits have been executed in individual and expressionist styles. The critic John Berger has suggested in his essay 'No More Portraits' from *Arts in Society* (1977) that the demands of modern vision are no longer compatible with the singularity of viewpoint that is the prerequisite for any static painted likeness. However, despite the theoretical reason for its demise it continues to emerge.

Changes in the structure of society in the last 100 years have emphasized the importance of all individuals, not just the royal, rich and famous.

With artists such as Max Beckman (1884 - 1950), Alberto Giacometti (1901 - 66), Francis Bacon (b 1910), Lucian Freud (b 1922) and David Hockney (b 1937), the portrait as a private interest has developed with little concern for accepted or traditional ideas and has enabled the artists to focus their attention on individuals without the pressure or constraints of the official commission. Ironically, since the 1960s it has become a mark of status to be painted by well-known artists purely because of their reputations.

Although there are now considerably more people painting and drawing than ever before, the portrait continues to be the least common art form among amateurs and professionals alike. However, what is painted is honest, and also expressive of the artist's personality or intentions. Commissioned portraits are often recognizably different in intention; the need to satisfy the client is likely to influence the way the portrait is approached.

A witty comment on the traditional concept of the portrait as a measure of social stature is apparent in a painting by Peter Blake (b 1932) entitled *Self-portrait with Badges*. The robes of office have been replaced by the contemporary uniform of blue denim and baseball boots, and a metallic shield of badges presents a compendium of references to popular culture. During the 1960s a number of artists, usually grouped as Pop artists, reacted against the mainstream development of painting since 1945 by celebrating the transience of contemporary culture. Appropriately, London and New York played prominent roles in its development and, because of its figurative orientation, an ironic return to an earlier conception of portraiture emerged. In contemporary culture the myth surrounding the early death of film stars has been perpetuated by the widespread familiarity of their images through photography. Andy Warhol (b 1930) is unique among contemporary painters in providing a kind of twentieth-century society portrait. Instead of popes or aristocrats, Warhol celebrates the contemporary heroes of stage and screen and has become the chief exponent of the posthumous portrait, silkscreened in multiple groupings of repeated images. The banality of the image of Marilyn Monroe, for example, is alleviated by the addition of paint applied in a cosmetic manner, with no attempt to enhance the volume of the head. A swathe of colour across the mouth doubles as lipstick and also comments on the more liberal use of paint by his American predecessors. The resulting portraits have nothing to do with observing an individual, but instead they rely on the spectator's familiarity with the subject's face or public image. In this respect they compare with the images of Caesar Augustus as seen by the general public during the Roman era and return the history of portraiture to its beginnings two thousand years ago.

RIGHT **Celia in Black Slip and Platform Shoes '73**, David Hockney. With a confident use of line and colour, Hockney has portrayed his subject in an informal, reclining pose. She is probably not totally relaxed, and the artist has captured this transience briefly and precisely. It is amusing that the hair looks almost like a child's scribble under scrutiny.

BELOW **Marilyn**, Andy Warhol. Multiple images have been silk-screened to create this portrait. The simple, abstracted forms for Marilyn's mouth, nose, eyes and hair make no attempt to convey her character; however, when the shapes are mentally combined with the well-known public image of her vulnerable, glamorous beauty, the result is a twentieth-century icon.

LEFT **Self-portrait with Badges**, Peter Blake. Painted in 1961, when the artist was 28, the portrait is iconographic with its multitude of references to Blake's life and influences and the 1960s. The collection of badges in itself reflects Blake's preoccupation with collecting odd bits and pieces, what he called 'durable expendables', including bus tickets and chip packets, some of which he involved in other pictures of the period. He was an Elvis Presley fan, and the inclusion of the pop star's 'photograph' indicates Blake's ability to represent precise likenesses and has the effect of dating the portrait. Blake became a leading figure of the Pop movement; he managed to sum it up in his work and simultaneously provide further inspiration for it.

THE HUMAN FIGURE

It might be thought that the portrait painter need only concern himself with the face, but this is a mistaken view. It should be understood that one particular part of the figure can only be isolated if it is first considered in relation to the whole. Similarly, although some knowledge of the skeleton is necessary, its useful application for the artist is dependent on knowing that this internal scaffolding allows the body to move, and in reality the bone structure will never assume the limp posture of the medical student's hanging skeleton. The figure is a living, moving whole, and the sense of life should always be borne in mind.

Although knowledge of man's internal structure was evident before the Renaissance, it had not been documented visually with the kind of accuracy that can be seen in the work of Leonardo da Vinci, who was working in the fifteenth century. Curiosity, coupled with a desire to draw and paint a convincing representation of a human being, resulted in Leonardo's remarkable exploration into the mechanics of the human body. The knowledge of anatomy acquired by artists of Leonardo's generation resulted in remarkably accurate depictions of the human body. The artist's skills in draftsmanship were essential as a means of recording anatomical complexity, and medical knowledge was closely aligned to artistic endeavor at that time. During the twentieth century the use of photography has enabled medical science to dispense with artistic skills, and although diagrams are still vital, artists are no longer needed to make intense observational drawings in the manner that was previously necessary. The vast array of modern medical textbooks enables anyone to study the mechanism of the human form, and the present attitude in art school no longer attaches such importance to the first-hand knowledge that was considered essential. It is ironic that Leonardo da Vinci knew more about the working of the human body than most twentieth-century artists.

Understanding the human anatomy involves the study of a complex structure of living organisms. The aims of the artist are, however, understandably different from those of a medical student and it is more useful in this book to consider the fundamental mechanics of the human frame rather than analyze the body from a clinical or biological point of view. The artist is primarily concerned with the aspects of anatomy which directly relate to what is visible to the naked eye. Because the shape of the human form is conditioned by the internal structure, it is necessary to consider the bones and

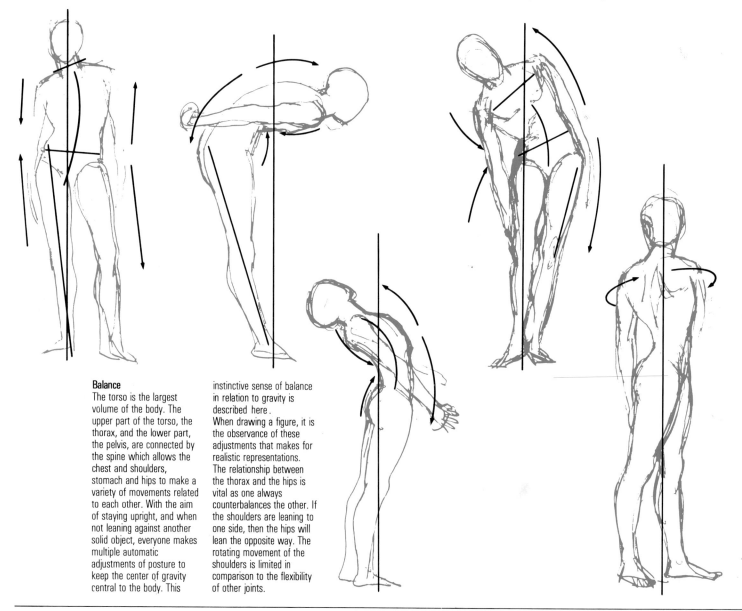

Balance
The torso is the largest volume of the body. The upper part of the torso, the thorax, and the lower part, the pelvis, are connected by the spine which allows the chest and shoulders, stomach and hips to make a variety of movements related to each other. With the aim of staying upright, and when not leaning against another solid object, everyone makes multiple automatic adjustments of posture to keep the center of gravity central to the body. This instinctive sense of balance in relation to gravity is described here.
When drawing a figure, it is the observance of these adjustments that makes for realistic representations. The relationship between the thorax and the hips is vital as one always counterbalances the other. If the shoulders are leaning to one side, then the hips will lean the opposite way. The rotating movement of the shoulders is limited in comparison to the flexibility of other joints.

LEFT **Sketchbook Drawings**, Leonardo da Vinci. The relationship of the head to the chest is just as important as that of the chest to the hips because all parts of the body, unless supported, are continuously balanced with each other. The directions of movement always flow, as can be seen when any movement is captured on paper or canvas, and an extended limb or a bent torso is always counterbalanced by an adjustment of weight somewhere else. When drawing or painting a portrait, it is vital to consider these relationships. Leonardo da Vinci made extensive researches into the human anatomy and his confident, realistic studies remain both anatomically and aesthetically interesting for the twentieth-century student. The head of the subject portrayed here is well placed on the shoulders. The most visible of the shoulder and chest muscles is the pectoralis major which is attached to the clavicle and the sternum and looks like a fan, when outstretched. It attaches at the other end to a point beneath the deltoid muscle on the arm. The trapezius is the muscle that runs down the back of the neck and attaches to the upper spine at the back and to the clavicle at the front of the torso.

muscles which in turn affect and dictate the surface shape.

The relevance of anatomical knowledge for the figurative artist is directly related to its application; consequently, an understanding of the nature of form is only of use if it is considered from a sculptural point of view with an emphasis on three dimensions. Every object can be described in terms of its internal structure. In most instances this is immediately apparent but occasionally, as in the case of the human form, it may be disguised by the nature of the surface covering, the skin. Gravity determines how the structure of an inanimate object rests on a surface and all geometric objects except those with curved surfaces — the sphere, the cone and the cylinder — will always remain static unless affected by some external force. However, the human form cannot be so easily understood: it must be considered anatomically as well as in relation to the force of gravity. Even if a figure appears static, it will only remain so if it supports itself by a balanced distribution of load or if its weight is acting against some other support.

If the skin, muscles and organs are removed from a body, the skeleton can only reveal the relative size and proportion of its constituent parts. It does not enable the artist to consider how the figure balances on the ground or how the movement of one part of the body results in a redistribution of weight in order to accommodate that move without loss of balance. When a particular part of the figure is moved it is the result of the muscles of the body affecting the skeletal joints in the way that a pulley provides the link between the otherwise static parts of a machine. If a person stands still for any length of time it is unlikely that he or she would choose a stiff symmetrical posture. Instead, the body is able to shift the weight from one side to another and at any given time one leg may be taking more weight than the other. This distribution of weight affects every other part of the figure, and unless the figure is affected by an external force it usually retains an instinctive balance.

Human anatomy
The skeleton
Apart from providing protection for the internal organs of the body, the skeleton provides shape and support for the figure as a whole. The word 'skeleton' is derived from the Greek word meaning 'dried up' and the properties of flexibility in the bone structure of a human being are quite different from those found in a living skeleton. While it is part of a living being, bone is constantly renewing itself. The unique structure of the human skeleton comprises 206 bones fitting together at joints which allow freedom and versatility of movement and yet still provide a strong and rigid framework for the body as a whole. A baby is born with 350 bones; many of these fuse together, and by the end of the growth period (at the age of 25 in men, younger in

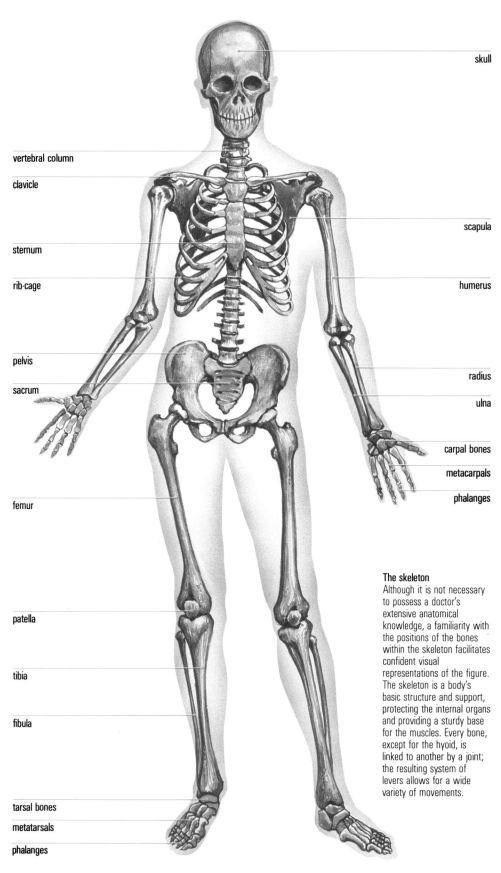

skull

vertebral column

clavicle

scapula

sternum

humerus

rib-cage

pelvis

radius

sacrum

ulna

carpal bones

metacarpals

phalanges

femur

The skeleton
Although it is not necessary to possess a doctor's extensive anatomical knowledge, a familiarity with the positions of the bones within the skeleton facilitates confident visual representations of the figure. The skeleton is a body's basic structure and support, protecting the internal organs and providing a sturdy base for the muscles. Every bone, except for the hyoid, is linked to another by a joint; the resulting system of levers allows for a wide variety of movements.

patella

tibia

fibula

tarsal bones

metatarsals

phalanges

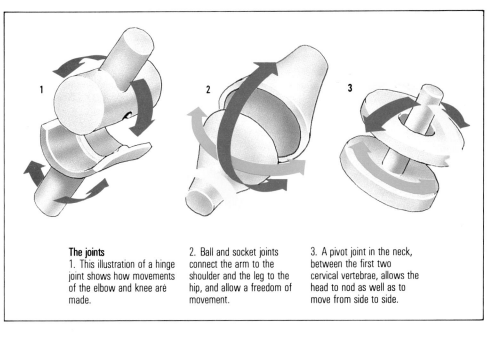

The joints

1. This illustration of a hinge joint shows how movements of the elbow and knee are made.

2. Ball and socket joints connect the arm to the shoulder and the leg to the hip, and allow a freedom of movement.

3. A pivot joint in the neck, between the first two cervical vertebrae, allows the head to nod as well as to move from side to side.

women) all bone fusion is complete and the skeleton assumes a reasonably permanent shape.

The human skeleton can be subdivided into two main areas known as the axial skeleton and the appendicular skeleton. The axial skeleton comprises the central axis of the figure and includes the bones of the cranium and face, the spinal column, the ribs and sternum. From these bones is attached the appendicular skeleton comprising the shoulder girdle, the arms and hands, and the pelvic girdle, the legs and feet.

Although the portraitist need not be concerned with the individual names of each bone it is useful to consider the individual characteristics of the various bone groupings. The spinal or vertebral column has a remarkable combination of properties and provides support for the weight of the torso and at the same time enables flexibility and considerable movement in many directions. In the foetus, the vertebral column can be seen as a single C-shaped curve of bone and yet after birth the raising of the head creates the beginning of the more complex curvature of the neck. Later the movement involved in standing and walking creates the beginning of a similar curve in the lower or lumbar regions. The curvature of the spine should never be underestimated in drawing, and a simple acknowledgement of its shape enables the artist to understand the main rhythms of a pose. Unless affected by injury, disease or poor body posture, the spine will always involve a subtle S-shape that is apparent when looking at x-rays or medical diagrams.

The bones of the lower extremities can be separated into three groupings involving the

cartilage

ilium

Cross-section through a hip joint

This diagram illustrates a cross-section through the ball and socket joint that connects the head of the femur bone to the ilium, a bone of the hip. Between the bones there are layers of cartilage which remove the possibility of friction until they deteriorate in old age.

femur

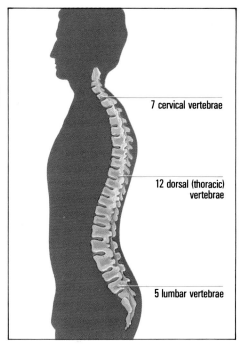

7 cervical vertebrae

12 dorsal (thoracic) vertebrae

5 lumbar vertebrae

RIGHT **Sketchbook Drawings**, Leonarda da Vinci. This extraordinary artist and scientist filled a great number of notebooks with observations and drawings of the human anatomy, sometimes carrying out dissections to increase his knowledge. The precise drawings on this page describe the bones and joints of the human arm from both sides. The shoulder-blade, or scapula, and shoulder are attached to the humerus of the upper arm by a ball and socket joint; the humerus attaches to the bones of the lower arm, the radius and ulna, with a hinge joint which allows great flexibility. The carpal bones of the palm of the hand are jointed to the lower arm and extend into the metacarpals and phalanges of the fingers. All Leonardo's observations are supported by notes in his curious mirror handwriting.

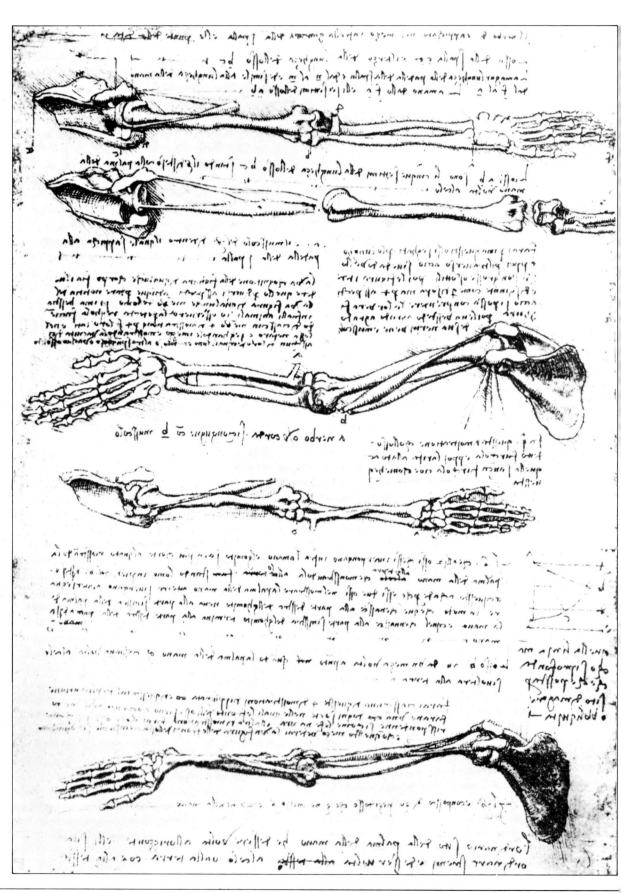

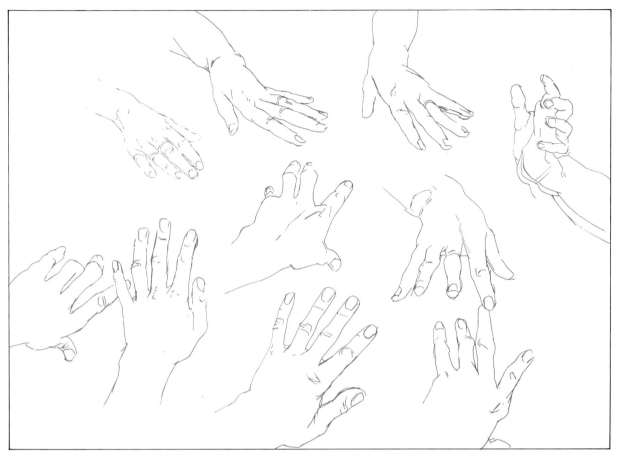

The hand
A complex series of joints in the hand make many combinations of movements possible. The flexible fingers of a healthy adult are capable of bending back some way over the top of the hand or of stretching across more than eight notes on a piano, while the other hand can simultaneously hold thin, fragile or moving objects of almost any shape, although there are limits as to size. When painting or drawing a figure, the artist soon becomes aware that hands are one of the most expressive features; Leonardo da Vinci was one of the first to notice and utilize this in his work. It is worth sketching them in different positions and from different angles to become familiar with the general form before incorporating them in paintings.

pelvic girdle, the bones of the legs, and the bones of the ankle and foot. The pelvic girdle supports the trunk and provides the casing in which the leg bones are attached. The adult pelvis consists of three separate bones fused together; the male pelvis is slightly bigger but generally narrower in its overall structure.

The femur or thigh bone is the largest and heaviest single bone in the body and it is important to realize that it is not in a vertical line with the axis of the erect body but is positioned at an angle. From a frontal view of the skeleton, the two femurs form a V-shape and because of the female's greater pelvic breadth the angle of inclination is greater than in the male. The patella or kneecap is a small flat bone lying in front of the knee joint and enveloped within the tendon that attaches to the large muscle of the upper leg. The tibia or shinbone is the larger of the two bones forming the lower leg, and the fibula or calf bone lies parallel with it on the outside of the figure. The ankle and foot are composed of the tarsal and metatarsal bones, and the toes are made up of bones known as phalanges. The general structure of the foot is similar to that of the hand, and yet the configuration of bones does not allow for the wide repertoire of movements associated with the hand.

The bones of the upper extremities of the figure can also be grouped into three units comprising the shoulder girdle, the bones of the arm and the bones of the wrist and hand. The pectoral or shoulder girdle is made up of two bones: the collarbone or clavicle and the shoulder-blade or scapula. They are important to the artist inasmuch as their movement visibly affects the horizontal axis of the shoulders and determines the position of the arms. The bones of the arms include one large bone from shoulder to elbow known as the humerus, and two thinner bones in the forearm known as the radius and the ulna. The construction of the arm is thus similar to the leg. The bones of the wrist are called carpals and the palm of the hand consists of five metacarpals which radiate from the wrist and connect to the phalanges of the fingers.

With the exception of the hyoid bone in the neck, to which the tongue is attached, every bone in the human form articulates with at least one other bone. The joints may be distinguished by putting them into three groups based on the amount of movement possible at the point of articulation. The least movable joints are called 'fixed joints', which category includes bones fusing together as they do in the cranium to create a suture. The next category includes joints which allow slight movement, such as between the radius and the ulna in the forearm. Freely moving joints, the third category, provide considerable freedom in different ways and these have more importance for the artist in that they determine the degree to which the body makes perceptible changes of position. Within this last category are other distinctions. A pivot joint connects the spine to the skull, whereas a ball and socket joint connects the femur to the pelvic girdle. These allow for considerable movement both sideways and vertically, whereas the hinge joint, as in the knee, is more limiting. Each joint is directly related to the kind of movement commonly made: the motion of walking or running is performed by strongly jointed bones able to carry weight whereas the joints of the wrist allow complex and delicate twists and turns which relate to the activities of the arm, hand and fingers.

At this point it is worth considering perhaps the most important part of the anatomy for the artist, namely the hand. The activity of drawing is made physically possible by the mechanism of this complex series of joints. In both structure and nervous connections, it is more highly advanced than in any other creature. It is simultaneously possible to hold a pencil between thumb and forefinger and yet at the same time grip an object with the palm and other fingers quite independently. Although the potential movements of the hand are complex, they are taken for granted. Even the simplest daily operations would be inconceivable without the use of

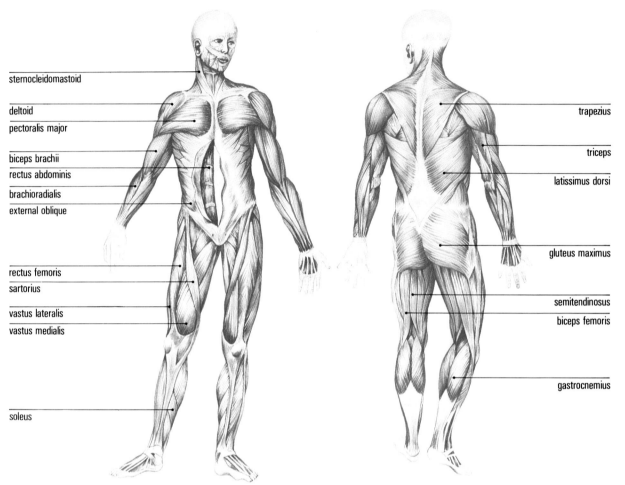

sternocleidomastoid

deltoid

pectoralis major

biceps brachii

rectus abdominis

brachioradialis

external oblique

rectus femoris

sartorius

vastus lateralis

vastus medialis

soleus

trapezius

triceps

latissimus dorsi

gluteus maximus

semitendinosus

biceps femoris

gastrocnemius

The muscles
These two diagrams are annotated to illustrate the positions of the main muscles of the anterior and posterior aspects of the body. The function of every muscle is to contract and relax in response to nervous messages, so causing bones and therefore the body to move, but they also assist in the circulation of blood and protect the visceral organs. Their main relevance for the artist is that their shape dictates the surface shape of the body; if an artist understands the muscles, and the direction they move in, the activity of observing a figure with the aim of reproducing it in two dimensions is made much easier.

this remarkable apparatus, which can touch every other part of the body. The hand has played an integral part in man's development. The activity of drawing and painting involves the coordination of hand and brain, and although the hand itself can only produce the physical results of observation, its versatility enables an artist to convey with remarkable subtlety the intention of the mind.

The muscles and skin
Linking the skeletal structure and the activity of movement is the function of the muscular system. All bodily movement is caused by the contraction or relaxation of some muscle group, and muscles can only work by pulling, and not by pushing. The engineering of the human body is such that in the physical activity of pushing against an object the muscles are in fact pulling against the joints.

Rather than consider the names of each muscular group, it is more important for the artist to recognize visually that they exist. As Jean August Dominique Ingres pointed out: 'Muscles I know; they are my friends, but I have forgotten their names'.

Most skeletal muscles are attached to two bones with the muscles spanning the joint in between; one bone usually moves more easily than the other. They are sometimes categorized according to the type of action they perform; for instance, muscles that bend a limb are called flexors and those which straighten a limb are called extensors. When considering the muscular structure of a figure it is important to remember that muscles are more evident if the figure is performing some activity, and in the many instances when a seated figure is observed, the bulk of the muscles will be relaxed. Strength is the result of the expansion of muscle fibre and not the addition to it; a strong person has the same number of fibres as a weaker person, and a person's complement of muscle fibre is determined at infancy and is consistent through life.

An important point in relation to the age of the sitter is perhaps best explained by one of the many observations made by Leonardo da Vinci in his study of anatomy: 'I remind you to pay great attention in making the limbs of your figures, so that they may not merely appear to harmonize with the size of the body but also with its age. So the limbs of youths should have few

muscles and veins, and have a soft surface and be rounded and pleasing in colour; in men they should be sinewy and full of muscles; in old people the surface should be wrinkled, and rough and covered with veins, and with the sinews greatly protruding.'

It is interesting that Leonardo considers the muscular structure in relation to the skin, and in reality our awareness of muscle is to some extent conditioned by the skin which reveals and conceals it. Taken as a whole, the human skin is the largest single organ of the body and is also the only unprotected tissue of the body which intervenes between the internal organs and the outside world. Its versatility matches that of the skeleton, it enables the body to retain fluid and it protects the body against contact with harmful rays while at the same time regulating blood pressure and body temperature. It constantly and efficiently renews itself and, more obviously, contributes towards forming the particular shape and colour of an individual. The colour of skin is affected by a dark pigment substance called melanin, the amount of which increases with exposure to strong ultraviolet light. Skin of whatever colour presents fascinating problems.

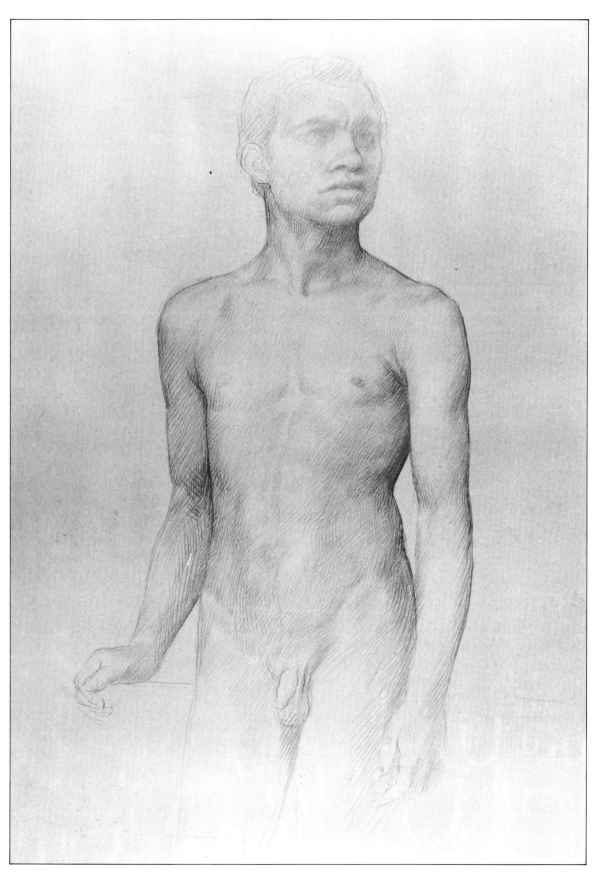

LEFT **Nude Male Youth**, Alphonse Legros (1837-1911). Born in France, Legros moved to England in 1863 and became a naturalized British citizen in 1881. He was well known for his engravings, and was made Professor of Etching at the Slade School, London in 1876. This etching displays his familiarity with the shapes beneath the skin. The neck and upper torso are drawn using hatching and crosshatching to describe the firm musculature. The sternocleidomastoid muscle attaches to the clavicle from above, while the trapezius and deltoid muscles of the neck and upper shoulders merge with the pectoralis major muscles across the chest. The latter attach to the sternum in the centre of the chest to form a thin, flat valley between the nipples. The rectus abdominis muscles, which run down the central panel of the torso below the chest, are separated by cartilage, so horizontal ridges are visible beneath the skin. The head and hips are faint by comparison with the detail of the torso.

RIGHT **Studies for Libyan Sybil**, Michelangelo Buonarroti. Drawn in red chalk, the main sketch describes the contours of a youthful back, with the bulged muscles left white to indicate highlights and broad and smudged lines worked in the shadows. The trapezius muscles down the back of the neck to the shoulder and centre back, the biceps and brachioradialis of the arm, the deltoid muscles of the upper shoulder and the slanting latissimus dorsi are all visible. The large gluteous maximus muscles curve away in relief. The bones of the spine and the rib-cage are also visible because of the stretching position of the arms. Brief sketches of toes, a hand and the shoulder help the artist to come to terms with the desired image in his mind.

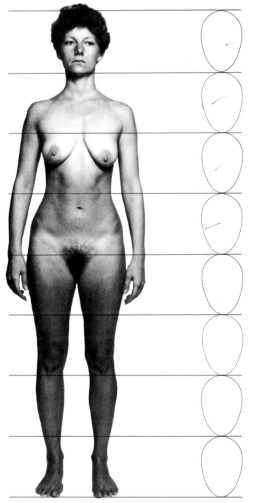

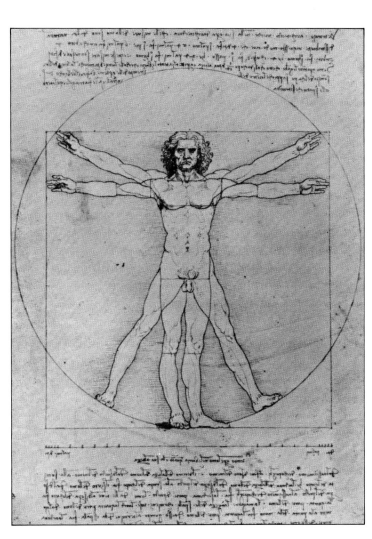

Proportion
It is useful to examine the relative size of the parts of the figure because scale and a sense of coherence are vital to a lifelike representation. It can be seen from the row of heads **(left)** that eight constitute the height of a standing adult. Leonardo's sketch, **Vitruvian Man (right)** demonstrates proportion in universal, geometric terms. The idea was taken from **De Architectura** by Vitruvius, which, expounding theories about the relation of man to his surroundings, principally architecture, is the only book of its kind to survive from the age of Antiquity. Leonardo displays the Renaissance concern to establish systems of scale and harmony similar to those of the Greeks, and places the image of a man within a circle and a square to illustrate the unique proportions of the human figure.

The skin is composed of two distinct kinds of tissue. The outer surface, visible to the eye, is known as the epidermis and consists of several layers of tissue that are continually being replaced by the innermost cells of this layer. The tissue beneath this is known as the dermis and consists of hundreds of nerve endings, sweat glands and hair roots. About one-third of the body's blood flows through this layer, and heat or motion affects the surface of the skin's colour by reddening its appearance. The entire body, with the exception of the palms of the hands, the soles of the feet and certain portions of the genitalia , is covered with hair, and even though this may not be always visible it is always affected by the muscular activity beneath the skin.

Life drawing
During this century the activity of drawing the nude figure, known as 'life drawing', has not involved much anatomical theory and there is a tendency to try to understand the figure as if it were simply a geometric object. During and after the Renaissance, artists equipped with anatomical knowledge were able to compose figures realistically from a preconceived repertoire, often using statues for models. Michelangelo had an extensive knowledge of anatomy, but this led him to draw figures in which the muscles were exaggerated to a degree unattainable in reality. In other words, each part of the figure was presented as though performing some activity requiring muscular force. Although Leonardo da Vinci realized that this was false, it became common practice for artists to depict muscular structure without any indication of muscular activity. Gradually, it has become common practice to draw figures using the experience gained through observation combined with a certain amount of preconceived knowledge.

The twentieth-century penchant for non-figurative art is mainly due to the influence of the Impressionist painters, in particular Paul Cézanne. Although Cézanne's training almost certainly included some direct anatomical research, his experiments with painterly problems of colour and form resulted in his indicating volume with planes, which indicate changes in surface direction. In this sense, Cézanne would consider the torso of a figure as a solid volume comprised of a surface structure of many different flat planes rather than as a ribcage with muscle and skin stretched over it. Although this is an over-simplification, there is no doubt that Cézanne's attitude towards the depiction of the human figure was quite different in concept from that of previous artists.

An awareness of the anatomy may be most useful when considering a figure disguised by clothing. The portrait painter, in particular, will often be confronted with a figure in which the only evidence of observable anatomical structure is in the hands and head. It is, however, often necessary to decipher how the structure of the body is situated beneath the clothing as it is then easier to imply the solidity of the figure.

At this point it is worth examining the relative size of the parts of the figure so that they can be presented in scale and with coherence. Any guidelines relating to human proportion are necessarily theoretical inasmuch· as nature's peculiarities can never be accommodated by man's attempts to categorize them. A further reason for not dwelling on what is ultimately an idealized view of the human being is the fact that portraiture involves an awareness of an individual and as such is at odds with a preconceived notion that the size or shape of the human body can be understood in identikit terms. The most useful reason for studying the norm, however, is that it makes noticing the differences and the peculiarities, if they exist, easier.

The Ancient Greek and the Italian Renaissance artists favoured the use of the head as a unit of measurement; this was related to the rest of the figure in such a way that it occupied one-eighth of the total height of the figure. The sixteenth-century Mannerist painters preferred a more elongated figure which was sometimes more than nine head lengths to the total figure; however, the average is much nearer to eight head lengths. For reasons of convenience the head is often used in this way; once its size has been stated on the paper an approximate size of the rest of the figure may be realized quickly.

One of the most well-known examples of theoretical human proportion is evident in Leonardo's drawing based on the ideas of Vitruvius. Entitled *Vitruvian Man*, the drawing is concerned with the way in which the outstretched limbs of a man may be related to the perimeter of the geometric forms of the circle and square. The revival of the classical ideals of human proportion emerged with the Renaissance preoccupation with man's relationship to the world. By relating the organic structure of the body to the man-made structures in architecture and painting, the artist was able to consider size, scale and proportion with reference to the needs and requirements of the human being.

In practical terms the male adult is generally larger than the female and the muscles are more developed. The shoulders of the male are broad in comparison with the hips and the reverse is true in the female. Although the size of both males and females differs considerably, the proportions across the body are usually consistent with this general physical comparison. When the artist is confronted by a model it is helpful to consider how the internal proportions of the limbs are related, and although there are always exceptions to the rule it will generally be found that a tall thin person will have a consistent thinness of proportion through the trunk, neck and limbs, whereas a short stocky person will have a consistent thickness throughout.

When the theoretical unit mesurement of the head is related to the figure it is assumed that the figure is standing in an alert posture, whereas in reality the effect of tiredness often results in the weight compressing the figure in such a way that the spine bends and the head sinks. When drawing a standing figure it should be apparent that the weight of the figure is taken by the legs and that the feet are firmly flattened on the floor. In an adult the hips are midway between the top of the head and the feet. If the head is then used as a measure of length it will be found that there is a

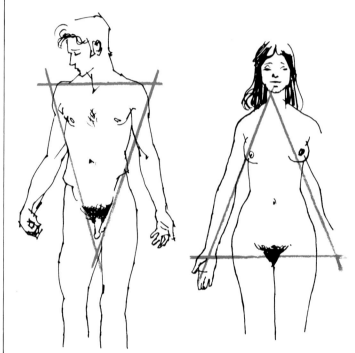

Male and female form
It is interesting to see how the male and female forms differ in these generalized sketches. Taking only the torso into account and ignoring the legs, the broad shoulders and thin hips of the idealized male figure form an inverted triangle, while the wide shallow pelvis and narrow sloping shoulders of the female can be seen as a pyramid shape. There is generally more fat in this area of the female, which accentuates the shape of the bones beneath. It would be ridiculous, however, to assume that all male and all female figures conform to a standard shape. The value of diagrams such as these is in prompting an awareness of general shapes which, in turn, make it easier to spot the peculiarities of individual figures.

similar distance from the bottom of the chin to the nipples. From the nipples to the hips will be two head lengths and again from hip to knee and knee to foot. The arms may also be considered in this way: shoulder to elbow will be one and a half heads and elbow to wrist one and a quarter heads. Although it must be emphasized that this is only an approximation, the relative proportions of arms and legs is usually the same in most people.

When the artist is confronted with a subject it is not usual to be concerned with reasons for certain aspects of growth, but it may be useful to consider that from a resulting drawing or painting the spectator will be expecting certain clues relating to the age of the model. Although the face reveals most of the information, the posture and activity of the body generally contributes to the feeling and mood that the drawing conveys. It should also be remembered that all human beings are at all times growing and changing and this aspect of life cannot be ignored.

During the first 18 years of a human being's life the rate of growth may appear to be considerable, but gain in weight is much slower than in most other animals. Even during adolescence the increase in appetite results in a relatively low increase in weight and a gain of 12 pounds or so per year is average. The normal height increase for boys is about three and a half inches in a year, and about two and a half inches for girls. The development of the skeleton is complex and corresponds to the growth and function of the internal organs of the body. At birth the bones are soft, comprised of connective tissue which

becomes cartilage and finally bone tissue. The top of the skull is soft and pliable at birth and any effects of distortion during birth disappear shortly afterwards. The most noticeable change in skeletal structure occurs as the bodily functions develop. At birth the neck is short, the shoulders are high and the chest is round. Gradually the neck lengthens and the shoulders and chest lower themselves as the ribs slope downwards. Pubescent developments cause a boy's shoulders and chest to strengthen and a girls's hips to widen. A 'shrinking' often occurs in old age, but this is not due to the bones decreasing in size.

Leonardo da Vinci was aware that apart from the physical signs of age manifesting themselves in anatomical structure, body language, indicated by different technical methods on paper or canvas, could also convey the age of the sitter. He wrote in *Treatise on Painting*: 'Little children when sitting should be represented with quick, irregular movements, and when they stand up, with timid and fearful movements.' These varying techiques would reflect the mood or actions of the subject. In its most extreme form, body language may convey emotion in the same way as facial expression. The posture of an adult will be understandably different from that of an old or very young person and for the portrait painter the selection of posture will be partly out of choice and partly necessity. The position of the body and the mood conveyed in it are important aspects of portraiture, enhancing the emotions contained within the picture and making the portrayal more convincing.

1

3

4

2

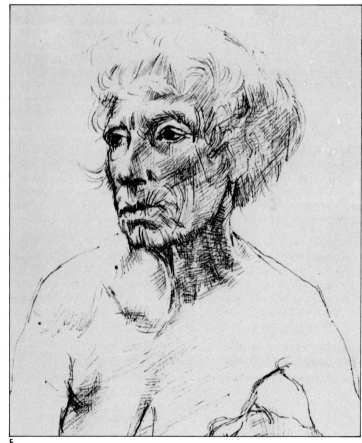

5

The effects of age

The artist should consider the medium, the composition and the pose carefully before making a life drawing. Each of these components have decisive effects on the look of the resulting picture.

1. **Saskia** is a quick, impromptu sketch of a small baby with alert, staring eyes drawn in ballpoint pen on thin notepaper. The brevity of the sketch and the scribbled shading match the jerky, uncontrolled action of a baby moving, while the dark pupils are the focal point of the portrait.

2. **Crouching Boy** is a similarly brief sketch drawn in soft pencils. The contours of his limbs, positioned askew, reflect the extraordinary agility of young children.

3. **Man in Blue Shirt** is more solid because the forms are filled in watercolour. A number of different tones, laid separately, give an impression of smooth, unlined skin by marking simple highlights and shadows.

4. **Seated Woman**, by comparison, displays a skin just beginning to lose its elasticity. The area of the face is interestingly filled with a whole range of tones, and lines under the eye and round the mouth are highlighted and shaded. In pastels the artist was able to effectively describe her pose and the texture of her skin.

5. This shows a detail from **Old Woman**, which was drawn using a ruling pen. The fine lines are exploited to portray a wrinkled skin, while the woman's position and sloping shoulders illustrate tired muscles.

THE FACE

Although there are more than two million species of life-forms on this planet, there is only one species of human being. Men and women are unique in the animal kingdom for many reasons, not least the ability to reveal a tremendous range of feeling and emotion by slight movements of facial muscle. Even without speech, people can communicate by almost imperceptible movements of the eyes, eyebrows, mouth or cheek.

From early childhood it is understood that certain states of feeling can be described through expressions. A picture of a person smiling or frowning usually involves an emphasis on the shape of the mouth with its upward or downward curve; the use of masks in the circus or theatre provides an audience with a similar repertoire of facial conventions. In both children's drawings and masks the shape of the actual features of the face provides clues about expression. Although the portrait painter will not usually be concerned with such obvious extremes, it is useful to understand how the features are affected by what lies beneath the surface.

The structure of the human head is such that any movement of the eyebrows, eyes or mouth is the result of muscles pulling across the face in many directions. A movement of the eyebrows affects the skin of the forehead, and in a similar way, a movement of the mouth affects the skin around the nose and chin, and also pulls the skin tautly across the bone structure of the cheeks. A certain amount of time is required to draw or paint facial expressions, but the very nature of human expression involves constant movement. Few artists have been able to convey pronounced states of facial expression because of the difficulty involved in arresting movement, and consequently many portraits display a less overt expression which is not designed to show any specific emotion but is often interpreted as one of melancholy or seriousness, although this may not have been the artist's intention.

Among the many well-known portraits, those by Frans Hals qualify as successful descriptions of facial expressions. Few painters have been able to capture with such apparent effortlessness the elasticity of the animated expression. By comparison, the paintings by Jan Vermeer convey a sombre view of reality, but on closer scrutiny also reveal a deep insight into the use of facial expression and an understanding of the almost imperceptible movements that imply life. The mouth, for instance, often looks moist and is usually slightly open as though in the process of drawing breath. The eyes also have a moistness which may sometimes reveal a quizzical expression simultaneously with a calm and reflective one. Within an apparently limited format Vermeer achieves a remarkable degree of subtlety, and any written description of the qualities of his paintings will be inadequate when faced with the work itself. Only the activity of observing and practising, combined with some anatomical knowledge, can provide the artist with the necessary understanding and skill to convey the complexity of human appearance with conviction.

Anatomical features
The skull
The skull can be divided into two main areas, consisting of the cranium and the facial bone structure that houses the cavities for the features of the face. The 28 bones which make up the human skull are all firmly connected with one another, with the exception of the mandible or jawbone. The hyoid bone is often described as being part of the skull, but in fact is the only bone in the body which is not attached to another. It is positioned in the upper neck.

At birth the head forms a much greater proportion of the total body length than in adults, and also the cranium occupies a larger proportion of the volume of the head than it does later. The cranium provides protection for the cavity that houses the brain and is comprised of thin curved plates of bone which in the newly born are separated by fibrous tissue at their edges. In the first year of life the bones grow and fuse together to form a rigid protective casing. The frontal bone of the cranium consists of a vertical section which forms the forehead, and a horizontal section which is divided in two and forms the roof of each eye cavity. Across the top of the head the frontal bone meets with the parietal bones, one each side, which in turn meet with the occipital bone at the rear of the skull. On each side of the skull there are two more plates of bone which are called the temporal and sphenoid bones. The two most prominent cavities of the face are the orbital, or eye, cavities. At birth they are proportionally much larger than in an adult, and from their upper border to the lower edge of the jaw is about a half of the total height of the skull. In an adult this measurement is about two-thirds of the total height because, as the teeth develop, the jawbone becomes more pronounced and the face becomes longer to match the cranium. The orbital cavities provide protection for the eyeballs; at their lower edge they are bordered by the zygomatic and maxilla bones which in turn provide the boundaries for the nasal cavity. Below the anterior nasal spine, the two maxillae meet and form the structure which contains the upper teeth.

All the bones in the face and cranium are firmly joined together with the exception of the mandible or jawbone, which is horseshoe-shaped. The jaw is attached to the cranium at a joint just in front of the ear. The human ears do not contain any bone and they are only evident in the skull as small holes behind the joint of the jaw. Of particular importance to the artist is the nodule of bone just behind and below this opening for the ear. This is called the mastoid process, and from this point the blatant sternocleidomastoid muscle of the neck emerges and runs diagonally down to the clavicle.

The position of the jaw in relation to the rest of the head is determined by the growth of the teeth and therefore also by the loss of teeth. In the mature adult the jaw is prominent and often in the male squarer and slightly larger, although it is dangerous to generalize. The ease with which a person's bone structure is visible is directly related to the age, sex and racial origin of that person. The skull of an infant differs considerably from that of an adult, and much of the excess skin tissue around the cheeks camouflages the facial bone structure which will become more prominent as time goes by. With old age the skin tends to sag, lose its elasticity and become thinner while the bones seem to be nearer the surface.

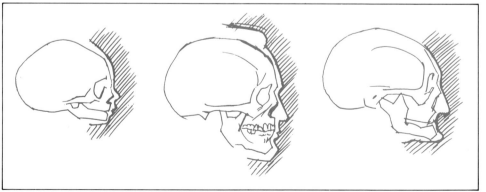

An ageing face
An awareness of the bone structure beneath the skin is vital, and it is interesting to notice the changes that take place between infancy and old age. These changes can be generalized and applied to almost any face. Within the first year of life, the bones of the cranium, separate at first, grow and fuse together. In infancy the eye cavities are proportionately larger in the skull than later in life, while the jawbone is undeveloped because there are few teeth. When the teeth grow the jaw becomes more prominent, so lengthening the shape of the whole face. Although adult bones do not usually change shape, the way that they are related or connected may, as cartilage dries and does not restore itself in old age. This causes a 'shrinking' effect. In the skull, teeth loss causes the jaw to recede.

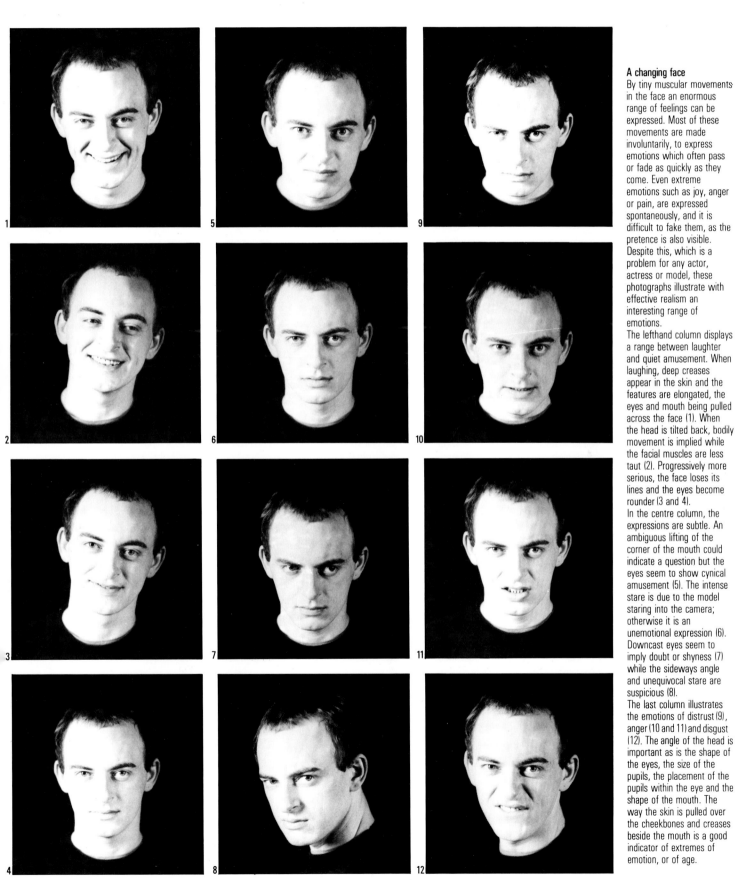

A changing face
By tiny muscular movements in the face an enormous range of feelings can be expressed. Most of these movements are made involuntarily, to express emotions which often pass or fade as quickly as they come. Even extreme emotions such as joy, anger or pain, are expressed spontaneously, and it is difficult to fake them, as the pretence is also visible. Despite this, which is a problem for any actor, actress or model, these photographs illustrate with effective realism an interesting range of emotions.

The lefthand column displays a range between laughter and quiet amusement. When laughing, deep creases appear in the skin and the features are elongated, the eyes and mouth being pulled across the face (1). When the head is tilted back, bodily movement is implied while the facial muscles are less taut (2). Progressively more serious, the face loses its lines and the eyes become rounder (3 and 4).

In the centre column, the expressions are subtle. An ambiguous lifting of the corner of the mouth could indicate a question but the eyes seem to show cynical amusement (5). The intense stare is due to the model staring into the camera; otherwise it is an unemotional expression (6). Downcast eyes seem to imply doubt or shyness (7) while the sideways angle and unequivocal stare are suspicious (8).

The last column illustrates the emotions of distrust (9), anger (10 and 11) and disgust (12). The angle of the head is important as is the shape of the eyes, the size of the pupils, the placement of the pupils within the eye and the shape of the mouth. The way the skin is pulled over the cheekbones and creases beside the mouth is a good indicator of extremes of emotion, or of age.

Bones and muscles of the face

These artist's drawings describe how the bones and muscles work together beneath the skin to form the exterior of a face as it is generally recognized. It is interesting to see how the flesh sits over the bones of the cranium, and transforms the macabre aspect of the skull into familiar features (1). The repeated angle of the head and skull illustrates how the shape of the nose and the thickness of the flesh are the main reasons for the actual shape of a face being different from the structure beneath (2 and 3). It can also be seen how the muscles affect the way the flesh moves. The frontalis muscle is the main reason for eyebrows moving up and down and creases appearing in the forehead. The mouth is capable of moving sideways as well as up and down, because of the buccinator and the muscles of the orbicularis oris, which include the levator anguli oris and the depressor anguli oris. The sternocleido-mastoid, which attaches to the mastoid process behind the ear and to the clavicle or collarbone beneath platysma, is a vital link between the head and the body (4, 5 and 6).

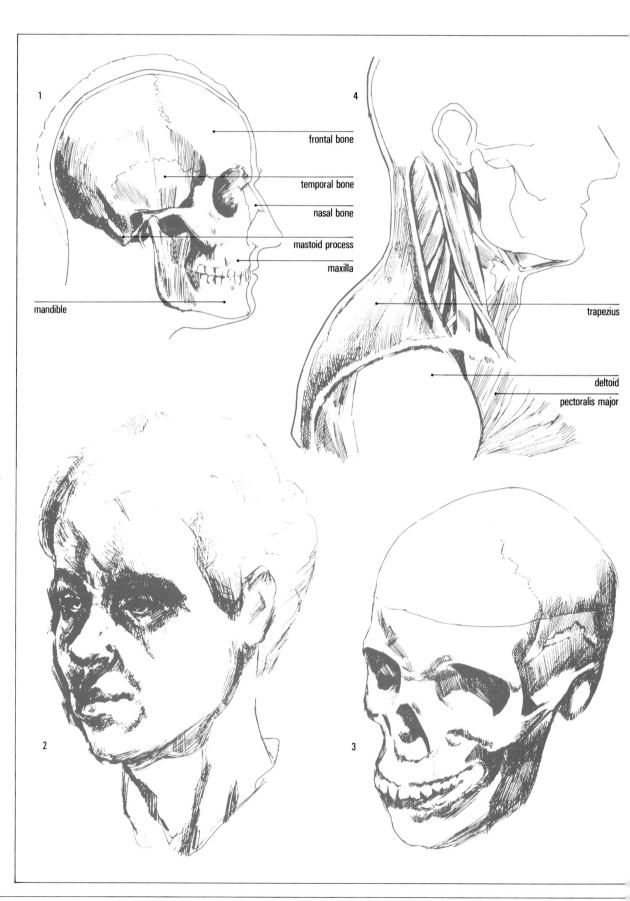

frontal bone
temporal bone
nasal bone
mastoid process
maxilla
mandible
trapezius
deltoid
pectoralis major

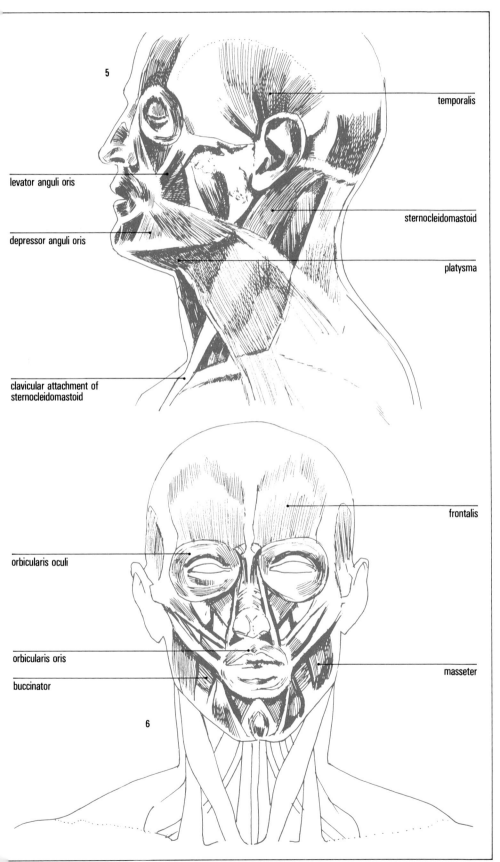

5

temporalis

levator anguli oris

sternocleidomastoid

depressor anguli oris

platysma

clavicular attachment of
sternocleidomastoid

frontalis

orbicularis oculi

orbicularis oris

masseter

buccinator

6

The muscles

The portraitist is primarily concerned with conveying character through the human physiognomy, and although the skull determines an individual's physical shape, it is the movement of the parts of the face which affects an understanding of individuality and uniqueness. In the nineteenth century, Realist painters attempted to describe the physical characteristics of individuals in great detail. During their student days they followed a standard procedure which involved examining a range of human expressions by copying schematized heads which displayed the exaggerated facial movements inspired by laughter, pain, rage or anger. The problem concerning the rendering of such feeling is that unlike the muscles of the body, facial muscles are usually only evident when they affect the features, but whenever the features move they do so in relation to certain other parts of the face.

The muscles which are used to create facial expressions are found under the skin of the face, under the scalp and in the front of the neck. They are directly related to the orifices in the skull and therefore centre around the mouth, the nasal cavity, the eyes and the external ears. Many muscles are responsible for lip movements: the orbicularis oris muscle which surrounds the mouth consists of a number of muscles entering the upper and lower lips from above and below respectively. Muscles also pass into each lip horizontally, and the buccinator muscle passes from the side of the mouth and into the cheek. All the muscles that affect facial expression are related to, and owe their movement and normal symmetry and control to the seventh cranial nerve.

The orbicularis oculi muscle surrounds the cavity of each eye and its fibres affect the eyelids and allow the eyes to close gently or tightly. The eyes may also move as a result of the muscles in the scalp stretching the forehead and also as a result of the nose moving. The muscles surrounding the mouth provide the most obvious facial movement; by using a mirror it is apparent that this movement is most evident around the jaw, cheeks and chin, as the skin is pulled taut over the bone.

When the artist is considering the head it is important to think about how the neck is attached and how its movement affects the positioning of the head. The most important muscle of the neck passes from behind the ear to the inner part of the clavicle and is called the sternocleidomastoid muscle. The two muscles, one on each side, together allow the neck and head to bend forwards, and independently they allow the head to turn from left to right and the chin to tilt upwards. The muscle on the right side turns the head to the left and vice versa.

When faced with a living model, the artist's knowledge of the skull and muscles will only be of use if it can be given practical application. The

human skull is easy to draw in the sense that it can be understood in terms of changes in structural planes and cavities. The head of a living person is less easily understood because of the addition of hair and features as well as the layers in between the skin and the bone. Although it is often tempting to start by drawing the lips or eyes, it is always wise to bear in mind the main structural parts of the cranium and face. By considering the form of the cranium rather than the hair, and the cheekbone and jawbone rather than the features, the artist should be able to compensate for the natural desire to underestimate these in relation to the size of the whole. If each component is considered separately, the result will be disjointed because the relationships are difficult to judge.

The skin and hair
One of the most difficult problems confronting the portrait painter involves reconciling the solidity and structure of the head with the softness and elasticity of skin. To assume that the head is sculpted in solid masses is to inherit the danger of the image being statuesque rather than human; however, if the reverse occurs the figure will lack structure. To achieve the balance required is difficult and paradoxical.

In Western painting over the centuries the quality of skin in paintings of both males and females has tended towards generalization. The female skin has almost always been pale and translucent, nearly white in comparison with the male skin. Painters often exaggerated this apparent difference until it became a pictorial convention.Fashions have also tended to accentuate this distinction. The high forehead and plucked eyebrows common in fifteenth- and sixteenth-century portraiture reinforced the idea that the female face is smoother and paler than the swarthy male's. In reality it may be true to say that the female skin is softer than the male, but, more importantly, the color of any fair skin alters due to the effects of temperature and physical well-being. Although this may not be so apparent in darker skins, an inability to recognize changes is the only reason.

Climatic change and exposure to the sun are the most obvious causes of changes in skin color and texture. The accumulative result of many years of exposure to the elements is evident in the dryness of an old person's skin. Lines and wrinkles around the features are more prominent with facial movement, but when they exist in a motionless face they allow the artist to map the structure of the head with a degree of ease.

A common error in attempting to paint the face arises through the assumption that the head stops where the forehead meets the scalp. Even with thin hair the forehead must be seen to move under the mass of hair rather than joining flush with it. Regardless of the angle of view, it is always the case that the shape of the skull dictates the way the hair grows.

Many people have been puzzled about how painters indicate hair, considering the apparent difficulty of describing with line and shape something which is comprised of many thousands of parts. Albrecht Dürer was once asked if he used a special brush made for the sole purpose of rendering hair; it is perhaps quite reasonable for people who are not familiar with painting to assume that the degree of realism often achieved could only result from trickery. Dürer painted hair in much the same way as many other painters, by first considering the overall shape of the head of hair and then indicating the direction of growth. Although everyone knows that hair is not a solid, it is easier to consider it so while painting. If a sculptor were intending to carve from a piece of stone the head of a woman with long flowing hair, he would first need to consider the hair as a tangible volume rather than as a collection of tiny strands. In much the same way, a

FAR LEFT Detail of **Grotesque Heads**, Leonardo da Vinci. These ink studies illustrate Leonardo's preoccupation with form and his masterful descriptive powers. In old faces skin loses its elasticity with the result that creases and wrinkles form; also, if the skin loses its fleshiness the underlying bone structure becomes increasingly visible. Such characteristics of age or personality add to the individuality of any portrait. These particular faces, however, are hideous in their realism, and lead to a supposition that they were fashioned in Leonardo's imagination. Whether this was the case or not, he was obviously aware that the size and angle of the neck, and the relationship of the head to the body, which includes the matching of skin thickness and bone size, are vital to the realism of any portrait.

LEFT **A Grotesque Old Woman**, probably after Quinten Massys (1465/6-1530). The exaggerated degree of ugliness in this portrait seems unbelievable. The deliberate hideousness of the woman's long, misshapen face is emphasized with cruel irony by the fashionable hat, and implies that the artist found an inherent fascination in the nature of the grotesque. It has been suggested that the picture is not an actual portrait but a piece of social satire, although it is thought by some that the sitter was Margaret, Duchess of Corinthia and Countess of Tyrol. It is not easy to understand why anyone with such features would wish to record them.

RIGHT **Self-portrait**, Sir Peter Paul Rubens. Like Rembrandt and many other artists, Rubens painted his own face frequently, as an exercise in capturing emotions and expressions. In this self-portrait, the face betrays no characteristics of age, rather a jauntiness and youthful humanity. His full moustache, small beard and wavy hair add a pattern of their own to the portrait which might otherwise have been bland, as his face is without wrinkles. The direct gaze and lifted mouth display an endearing honesty and liveliness.

LEFT **John Maynard Keynes** (c 1908), Gwen Raverat. This is a relaxed but precise portrait sketch of the young Keynes, who was later to become a leading world economist. The profile and hair are drawn in pen and ink and ink washes, and a striking white highlight on his neck describes sunlight or a lamp behind him.

BELOW **The Head of Balzac**, Aubrey Beardsley (1872 - 98). Drawn for the front cover of a volume of Honoré de Balzac's collected work, **La Comédie humaine**, this is a strong, graphic likeness of the author. Beardsley's style and clear contouring suited the author's determination and individuality.

painter must first simplify the overall mass, which reflects and shades light.

Although a mass of curly hair may not reveal such obvious changes of colour in light as smooth, straight hair, it is always the case that more light is reflected on the top of the head if the figure is lit from above. If the hair stands away from the head as thick curly hair often does, the areas nearer the scalp will be denser and also darker, being shaded by the hair nearer the surface. Once the light source is established, changes in colour and tone can be noted. Eventually the mass may be made to resemble hair in the method of paint application. With age and loss of hair, the scalp becomes more prominent.

The eyes

Another difficult problem for the portrait painter involves the depiction of eyes. In many portraits they are the means by which an immediate confrontation with the spectator is made. Because of their obvious importance in any portrait, it is crucial that they do not become unrealistically prominent in relation to the rest of the face. It must be remembered that the eyeball is almost spherical and that the actual portion of its visible surface is small in relation to the area hidden by the eyelids and within the bony orbital cavity. The outer surface, or white of the eye, is called the sclera and consists of protective fibrous tissue. The front portion of the sclera is transparent and forms the cornea; this amounts to about one-sixth of the surface of the sphere. The curvature of the cornea is more convex than that of the sclera and might be considered as being a segment of a smaller sphere joined to the larger.

One of the most immediate characteristics of a person's face is the colour of their eyes, and this pigmented part is called the iris. It is situated behind the cornea and is comprised of radially arranged fibres and circular muscular fibres which alter the size of the black pupil in much the same way as the aperture mechanism of a camera lens. The pupil is in fact a hole; in bright light it contracts and in darkness it expands to allow more light through to the lens within, which is suspended by ligament and provides the crucial link with the light-sensitive part of the eye known as the retina. While seeing, images are focused on this inner surface, and depending on the distance involved the lens will alter its shape.

When objects nearer than about 20ft (6m) are observed, the anterior surface of the lens bulges forward and becomes more convex, allowing those objects to be received by the retina. In normal vision the slightly different images of the two eyes are combined by the visual cortex to enable stereoscopic vision.

In the adult face the eyes are situated midway between the top of the head and the bottom of the chin, with a space equal to the width of one eye between them. Unless the eyelids are deliberately forced wide open, a small portion of the iris is hidden by them; when the head is vertical, the top lid covers the top portion of the iris.

It is almost inevitable that the portrait painter focuses on the eyes, and yet when any part of the face is given too much prominence there is a danger that the part will destroy the unity of the whole. When confronted by a portrait by Rembrandt the eyes, painted without undue emphasis, appear to be like visual magnets, demanding attention. The adage that the quality of a portrait depends on whether the eyes follow the spectator around the room almost achieved credibility with Rembrandt's self-portraits, in which the intense and penetrating stare is a reminder of the intensity involved in the activity of painting a human presence. Although Rembrandt painted eyes with remarkable accuracy, he always managed to situate them in such a way that the orbital cavities of the skull seem to enclose and protect them.

The white of the eye, as it is known, is something of a misnomer; in reality its appearance is dependent on the state of the subject's health and on light, and often its moistness, indicated by highlights, will cause it to appear bluish-grey in colour. A cast shadow caused by the effect of light on the forehead will often accentuate the depth of the eye sockets and, under close scrutiny, it becomes evident that the eyelids themselves have a thickness which casts a shadow onto the surface of the eyeball.

Racial differences

Racial origin not only affects the skin pigmentation, but also the general shape of the body and face. Direct observation of particular individuals should dispel any notion that physical types can be easily categorized; within any one geographical loction there are always infinitely diverse physical differences which defy generalization. However, because the shape of the overlying skin and muscle tissue in any face is dependent on the underlying bone structure, some racial differences are reasonably apparent. The shapes of skulls vary, for example.

The history of Western portraiture is inevitably dominated with images of white Europeans, and yet even within this limitation there is a range of facial types. In 1740, Carolus Linnaeus, the Swedish taxonomist, suggested that the species *Homo sapiens* could be considered in terms of five distinct variations: African, American, Asiatic, European and Indian. By 1900 the groupings had become more complex and the French anthropologist Joseph Deniker suggested that there were in fact six groups with 29 smaller subdivisions of those groups. By 1961 W.C. Boyd, an American Professor of Immunochemistry, reached the conclusion through the use of blood groupings that a total of 13 groups make up the one species.

The definition of any one grouping is difficult and there can be no specific characteristics that are particular to any one particular race. In North America there has been an attempt to define the characteristics of both black and white people, assuming for the sake of simplicity that the white people are of western European origin and the black people from the Gulf of Guinea. It was discovered that the North American negro generally has a lower hairline on the forehead, a broader nose with a lower bridge, and a more pronounced jaw.

In the case of both white and black people being of similar stature, the negro will be the heavier, with a shallower chest, narrower pelvis and longer legs. The obvious difference

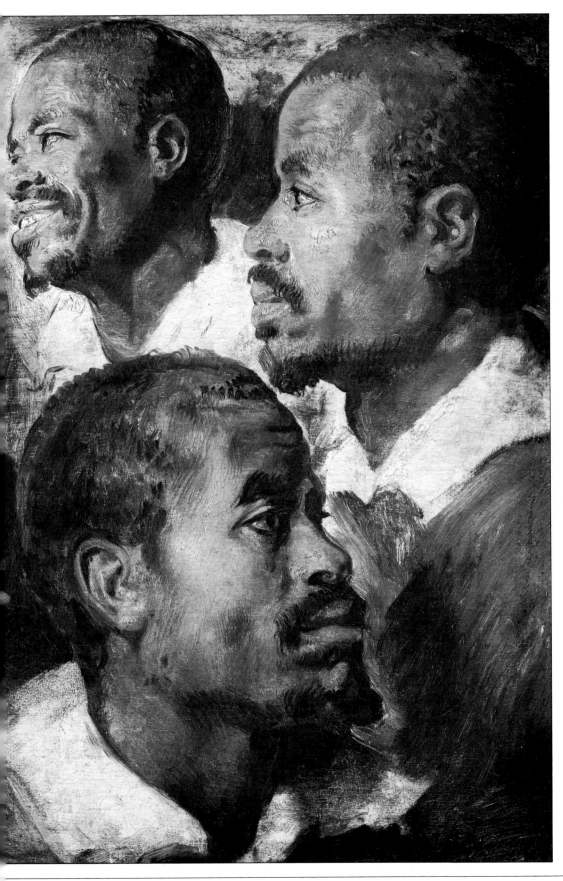

LEFT **Studies of a Negro Head**, Sir Peter Paul Rubens. This type of study – painting a number of different views of one face on the same canvas – was unusual for its time, and provides an animated composite portrait. It is interesting that not only do the views vary, but also the lighting and even the expressions differ for each of the four heads. The main study on the left is a three-quarter head-and-shoulders view but is made more unusual and dramatic because the subject is observed from a low position, the light coming up to illuminate the modelling on the side of the face, heightening the expression and the upward gaze. The topmost study is also a three-quarter view, but in this case the expression is more animated and the light is coming from the front, casting the back of the head into shadow.

The study which occupies the righthand corner is a classic profile view, the light being used to describe the contours and details of the face, rather than accentuate an expression. This provides a revealing contrast with the lower foreground study, where the lighting creates a more sombre mood. The composition, with the heads arranged in a circle, brings the four separate studies into a unified whole.

between people of different origin or race is the colour of skin, and as there is no recipe for painting skin tones, the artist must rely on powers of observation in coming to terms with the particular characteristics of each individual sitter, whatever his or her race, age or sex.

Using light to reveal facial characteristics

The earlier part of this chapter was concerned with the anatomical construction of the skull, muscles and skin but to apply these facts practically, the artist is reliant on direct observation of what is, in fact, only the outer surface. The existence of light and shade is the artist's most useful aid for the application of knowledge about the human form.

In Western painting the description of volume has often been attained by acknowledging a light source above and to one side of the subject. Many painters realized that the light source in a painting is most effective in a realistic sense if it mimics the natural light of the sun. As Leonardo da Vinci directed in his *Treatise on Painting*: 'Above all, see that the figures you paint are broadly lighted and from above . . . for you will see that all the people you meet out in the street are lighted from above, and you must know that if you saw your most intimate friend with a light from below you would find it difficult to recognize him.'

In nearly all Leonardo da Vinci's portraits the light source is consistent with his observation of the effect of natural light. Shadows cast from a consistent light source help to indicate the changes in direction or plane across the form. After Leonardo it became common practice to indicate the shadows of the nose and brow to explain the volume of the head. In a similar way the chin would cast a shadow across the neck, and the cheekbone furthest from the light source would be bathed in shadow. Leonardo's advice about lighting was connected with his realization that the emotional content of the picture would be to some degree the result of it. If the lighting were directed from below the face, the effect would be quite different; some artists have used this quality to their advantage, creating unusual, theatrical or dream-like results which automatically distance the spectator.

Edgar Degas was fascinated by the effects of artificial lighting and sometimes transferred the elements of theatricality into a portrait in a domestic interior. The following quotation, taken from *The Notebooks of Edgar Degas*, is an example of the advice he gave to others: 'Work a great deal at evening effects, lamp light etc. The intriguing thing is not to show the source of light but the effect of the lighting.' Degas realized that by not revealing the source of the light he could take more liberties with its effects. Many painters before Degas had used a single source of light; at first glance, a portrait by Rembrandt, for example, appears to present a

FAR LEFT **The Virgin and Child with St John**, Pietro Perugino (active 1469 - d 1523). Thought to have been a pupil of Piero della Francesca, Perugino was painting during the early Renaissance. This religious portrait displays some of the advancing ideas including the theory, later expounded by Leonardo da Vinci, that bodies should be lit uniformly from above. A diffused light bathes the three figures in their landscape setting, and soft shadows, particularly beneath the Virgin's chin, help to describe the volumes of the faces and the exact positions of the limbs.

LEFT **Portrait of a Woman**, Frans Hals. Painted c 1640, about 150 years after Perugino's portrait, this picture displays the use of interior lighting. There is one direct light source, which may have been artificial or from a window but has still been contrived to fall from above, in accordance with the convention that developed in the attempt to imitate nature. The light is deliberately strong and the woman's face more dramatically modelled as a result.

Directional highlights on skin
These images illustrate the effects of directed interior lighting on black and white skins, and should not be confused with the effects of daylight. The images are matched on the two pages. To begin with, a strong, narrow light was directed onto the necks of the models from behind them. It had the effect of whitening both skins where it shone, while it failed to provide any light to show the form of the rest of the head. The height of the sternocleidomastoid muscle created a shadow then a spot of light was caught on the jawbone (1).

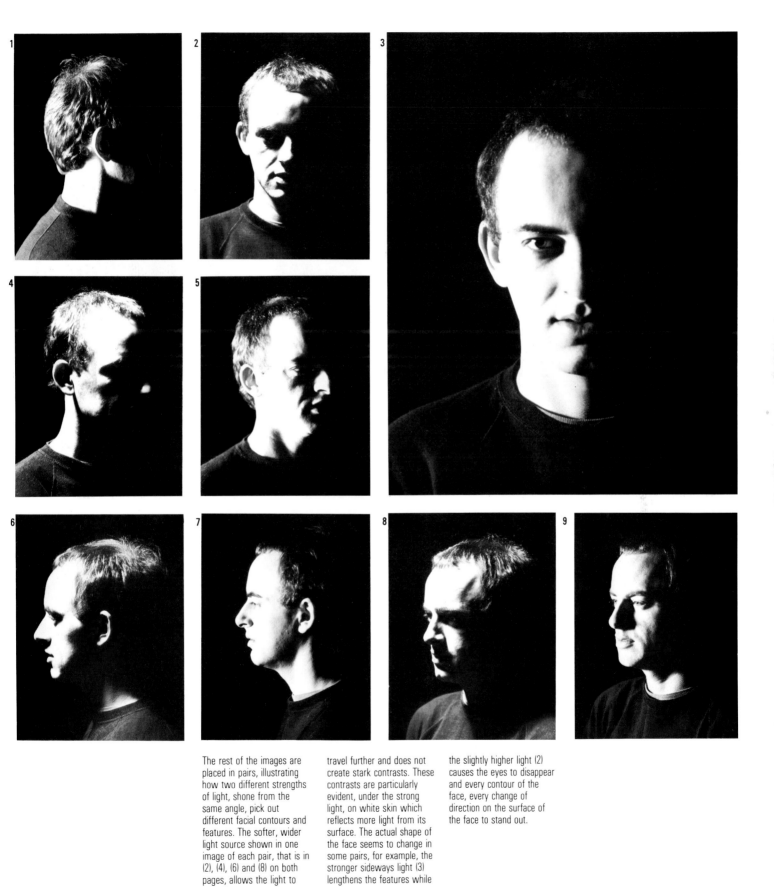

The rest of the images are placed in pairs, illustrating how two different strengths of light, shone from the same angle, pick out different facial contours and features. The softer, wider light source shown in one image of each pair, that is in (2), (4), (6) and (8) on both pages, allows the light to travel further and does not create stark contrasts. These contrasts are particularly evident, under the strong light, on white skin which reflects more light from its surface. The actual shape of the face seems to change in some pairs, for example, the stronger sideways light (3) lengthens the features while the slightly higher light (2) causes the eyes to disappear and every contour of the face, every change of direction on the surface of the face to stand out.

RIGHT **Self-portrait**, Jean Millet (1814 - 75). The lack of facial detail does not mean that there is a subsequent lack of character in this portrait. The hat pulled down over the artist's ears, thick clothing and a rough beard and moustache give a vivid impression of the artist's temperament. Born in a French peasant family, Millet started to depict **genre** scenes and country people in conditions of hardship and poverty. Drawn on rough-grained paper, the technique of this down-to-earth self-portrait matches the content. There is a dark shadow beneath the peak of the artist's hat while the rugged features, the nose and cheekbone are highlighted for a solid, chiselled effect.

LEFT **Self-portrait**, Piet Mondrian (1872 - 1944). Softly lit from above, the eyes in this portrait are emphasized, while the mouth and chin fade into darkness. Lines in the skin are given texture by the thick paint.

BELOW **Portrait of a Man.** The contours of this face are well described by this pen and ink technique of hatching and stippling in the shadows. Strong lighting in front throws the features into sharp relief.

figure bathed in light in much the same way that a figure might be observed in a darkened room with a shaft of light falling on one side. On closer examination it is apparent that Rembrandt did not feel it necessary to observe the logic of natural light and although his paintings are deceptively real, the light is allowed more emphasis in certain places for dramatic pictorial purposes. In order to draw attention to the face and hands, Rembrandt would accentuate the lighting in certain places. The problem with a pictorial convention, however, is that once it becomes an acceptable means of describing volume it is in danger of becoming a cliché. In the hands of lesser painters, Rembrandt's dramatic lighting became an arbitrary means of describing form.

The academic painters of the nineteenth century were trained to observe the effects of light on the plaster cast of a face, and it became common practice for them to paint a real person with a preconceived notion of how light would affect the face. In many instances the adherence to a pictorial convention probably passed unnoticed, but when the artist attempted to paint a portrait in a landscape setting there would often be a discrepancy between the convention of lighting on the face and the apparently natural effect of light on the landscape. The Impressionist painters dispensed with many preconceptions and the accepted mode of lighting a face was the first to perish. Edouard Manet deliberately chose to light his figures from the front and was often criticized for his rejection of *chiaroscuro*. By using light in this way Manet was able to flatten faces and concentrate on the subtle internal volumes without the use of cast shadows. People found it hard, at first, to accept Manet's paintings of figures with their apparently shadowless faces; in fact they are not flat at all.

In everyday life our perception of a human face often involves many different light sources at the same time and, similarly, the portrait painter may be confronted by a subject in which the directions of the light sources are various. This will cause a plethora of cast shadows and may provide problems for the artist attempting to come to terms with the volumes of a particular face. The most straightforward way to begin portrait painting is to limit the light sources for reasons of convenience, and later to experiment by changing or strengthening them.

Artificial light has its advantages, not least is the fact that its strength and position do not change. It is now possible for the artist to select a light source regardless of the quality of natural light or the time of day. Natural light, which changes minute by minute, can prove annoying for the portraitist attempting to capture a face in a certain light with particular shadows. In these circumstances, it may be worth taking a photograph of the subject and working from this until a similarly lit opportunity arises. If a strong, harsh light is required, providing distinctive shadows and modelling, a powerful tungsten bulb can be used and produces a brighter constant light than sunlight.

By comparison with the light bulb, natural light is bluish in colour. This difference can be observed while sitting in an underground train as it passes through a dark tunnel; the eyes become accustomed to the artificially lit environment and it is not until the train moves suddenly from the tunnel into daylight that the blueness of natural light is apparent. The celebrated north light, south light in the southern hemisphere, attracts artists who require a soft, diffused light because it does not cause harsh contours.

DRAWING THE PORTRAIT

Drawing as design

The twentieth century has seen many changes in the teaching of drawing, especially in the rejection of the laborious academic methods advocated before and during the nineteenth century. Before a student at art school was allowed to draw a model he was obliged to spend many hours working from a plaster cast. The study of anatomy and an understanding of the effect of light and shade was supposed to be the best way to prepare an artist for the more advanced problems of drawing a real person. Many artists did not emerge from this difficult training without succumbing to the pitfalls of academicism, but those who did are remembered for the more personal language that developed in spite of it.

Jean Auguste Dominique Ingres is often quoted as having said, 'Drawing is the probity of art', and yet the meaning of the word drawing in the English language cannot fully encompass its wider implications in other languages. In fact, in both French and Italian the word for drawing (*le dessein* and *il disegno*) also means 'design'. When Ingres was remarking on the importance of drawing he was not concerning himself with presenting visual facts in the form of a recognizable image, but was commenting on the necessity of organizing pictorial structures in such a way that the individual parts are considered in relation to the coherence and unity of the whole. The term 'drawing' as understood in English does not fully accommodate this meaning; this might partly explain the blinkered assumption that drawing should be connected with the imitation of reality.

Before describing the techniques of drawing, it is worth considering the uses and purposes which will affect how these techniques develop. Drawing with a line is the most immediate and primitive method of making an image and lends itself to making quick sketches or notations, which might have symbolic meaning. In Eastern cultures the calligraphic nature of writing reveals how closely linked drawing and writing can be, and yet in the Western world the division is pronounced. If an artist decides to make a quick study of a particular face the use of line emerges as a kind of shorthand, but with more time a different kind of drawing might emerge as the result of a thorough exploration into the volume of the head. The quality of a drawing is not necessarily improved by more work and quite often a lengthy study results in a lifeless image whereas a quick study appears lively and spontaneous. Sometimes a drawing may be considered as a complete statement in a creative sense, sometimes as a means of preparing for a painting; equally a drawing may be the visual document of objective, perhaps scientific, research and as such not relate at all to the procedure of painting.

Leonardo da Vinci provides evidence of the latter approach in his analytical studies of anatomical structure which were the visual

results of tireless research. It would be a mistake to assume that the nature of direct observation precludes creativity, but the degree to which it imposes restraints on the artist will affect the resulting drawing. If, for example, a technical draughtsman is required to draw the working components of an engine, the desire for clarity will take precedence over an artistic or creative use of line or shape. In this function the drawing is required as an acknowledgement of fact and as such will succeed or fail through the artist's visual explanation of those facts. The drawing technique is irrelevant.

When attempting to draw the human figure, such rigorous objectivity is unnecessary; however it is important first to understand the 'com-

ABOVE **Portrait of Jean Léger**, David Hockney. Executed in 1973, this pencil drawing shows a subtle combination of different types of mark, both linear and tonal. The basic structure of the portrait is linear, the lines being traced around the contours with precision and economy. A similar use of simple line in the gridded pattern on the trousers effectively suggests form. A restrained use of hatching provides tonal contrast but does not detract from the purity of the line. Darker shading on the nose serves to bring this feature forward in space; the darkest areas are the hair, eyes and watchstrap, balanced to give harmony. The result shows an interplay between the particularity of the subject and the volumes and depth of the figure.

ABOVE RIGHT **Caravaggio**, Octavio Leoni. This drawing relies on tonal contrast rather than a linear construction. The rich intensity of the dark areas suggests the famous artist's violent life.

ponents', as it were, of the figure in order to be able to express them competently with a degree of subjectivity later. Just as handwriting is expressive of personality, so is drawing. If several artists were to attempt to draw the same portrait, the results would be quite different. Even within the apparent limitations of one particular medium, the expressive nature of drawing is dependent on an individual's response to a given situation.

Learning to observe
During the course of day-to-day living, an awareness of visual phenomena is restricted to the recognition of certain clues that distinguish one object from another. Most people would be

able to describe with some accuracy the particular visual characteristics of another person. However, very few people would be able to translate that knowledge into a drawn image. When confronted with another person, an awareness of their appearance is to some extent due to the recognition of facial mannerisms or gestures, and attention is normally focused on the separate features. Consequently when first attempts are made to draw a figure, the features of the face are indicated and little or no attention is paid to the structure or complete form of the head.

One of the major problems encountered through drawing is thus connected with seeing. Children are usually curious about the visual

TOP AND ABOVE This modern portrait sketch was drawn in charcoal and Conté crayon using a photograph as reference. A comparison of the two indicates that the artist's intention was not to reproduce a strict likeness, but to suggest certain qualities of light. One of the difficulties of working from photographs is that the

drawing might turn out to be too static, but here the looseness and spontaneity of the charcoal medium confers a greater degree of liveliness than existed in the original photograph. Charcoal and crayon lend themselves well to the type of treatment where the accent is more on contrasts of light and shade than descriptive work.

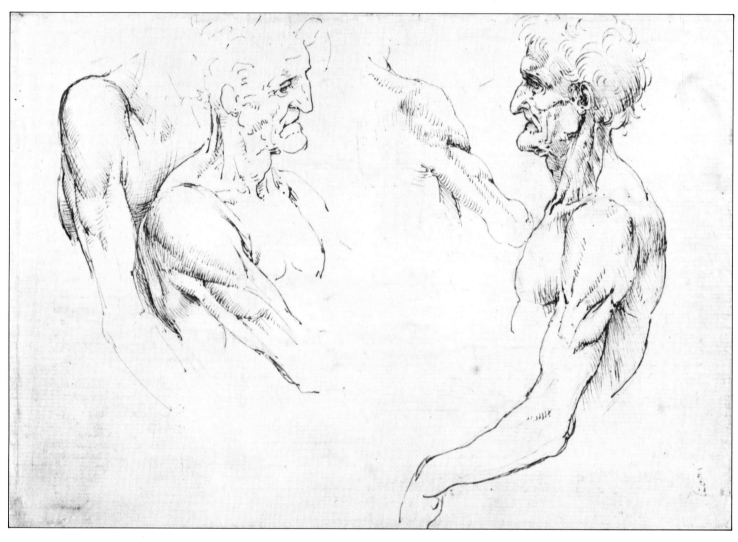

world and the images they make represent an unconscious attempt to find a symbol or sign to remind them or a viewer about the real world of people and objects. Their drawings are not hindered by any preconceived notions about representation and do not conform to any pictorial conventions. As a child becomes older, the innocence of such drawings becomes equated with naivety, and any art form that does not conform to a more realistic representation of the world is likely to be dismissed. It is a curious aspect of human development that drawing as a means of expression is common to children of all races and backgrounds, and yet with age the desire to continue making images becomes replaced by the verbal and written language.

The activity of seeing and observing with the final aim of transferring the image is complex. Most people who do not need to translate their observations into any tangible equivalent will find considerable difficulty in selecting from reality the most vital shapes and forms that collectively suggest a coherent image. In a face, for example, it is not just the shape of the eyes and

the mouth that are important, but the selected shape of the whole. Everybody who is gifted with sight will be able to distinguish a familiar face in a crowd, but few people would find it necessary to translate that image into another form, unless a verbal or written description of that person is required. When an artist attempts to describe a person visually he will need more information about that person and cannot rely solely on a familiarity with certain features.

Understanding the physical structure of bodies in space is the first problem of drawing; the second problem involves translating that understanding onto the two-dimensional surface of a sheet of paper. The third and perhaps most crucial factor in drawing involves getting rid of the common misconception that the merits of a particular drawing are somehow connected with the degree to which it imitates reality. Although this might seem to be a contradiction of intention, it is important that the artist's interpretation of reality is the product of a selective process and as such is directly related to the idea that a drawing will succeed or fail depending on

the strength of its own internal structure of lines and shapes. A constant awareness or acceptance of images through photographic reproduction has imposed restrictions on our visual development to such a degree that most people usually consider the merits of a drawing in relation to photographs and do not acknowledge the fact that a drawing may be interesting because of its own self-sufficient structure. In this respect, a person who is not used to studying the structure of objects will probably find it difficult to recognize the visual structure of a drawing unless it appears to mimic reality and include the visual superficialities that are required in the casual recognition of objects in everyday life.

Aspects of drawing
Form and line
The strength of a linear drawing depends on whether the internal volume of the figure or object is satisfactorily suggested by the line of its contour. In any linear drawing the surface area of white paper is considerably larger than the area of paper that is covered by the pencil

FAR LEFT **Head and Shoulders of a Man**, Leonardo da Vinci. Leonardo's drawings reveal a process of enquiry, both scientific and artistic; the outstanding beauty and precision of these works alone would qualify him as a great artist. Anatomy was a lifelong interest; his researches in this field led him to the brink of discovering, it is believed, the circulation of the blood. Leonardo pursued all of his studies determinedly, refusing to accept any fact or theory until it was substantiated by his own discoveries: in anatomy, for example, many of his detailed and annotated drawings were the result of his own observations of dissections. Leonardo drew in all media – red and black chalk, pen and ink, silverpoint – and accompanied his sketches, caricatures, plans and drawings with notes executed in mirror writing. After his death, the many notebooks containing his drawings passed into the hands of Pompeo Leoni who organized them into two volumes – one for science and one for art. In 1637 one of these volumes was given to the Biblioteca Ambrosiana in Milan; the other eventually became the property of the British Crown and is now in Windsor Castle. In the nineteenth century, 600 of these drawings were placed in separate mounts; the anatomical drawings were bound separately. Together these represent the most extensive documentation of Leonardo's extraordinary life of research and observation.

LEFT **Portrait of a Young Man**, Albrecht Dürer. This portrait was executed in charcoal and the crisp lines and subtle modelling display Dürer's skill as a draughtsman and his control of the medium. Today charcoal is regarded more as a medium suitable for sketching but this drawing shows it can be used for very detailed, highly finished work.

and the linear description of form requires an awareness of what appear to be the empty spaces between the lines. These lines do not delineate actual forms; lines in a drawing represent artificial boundaries. If, for example, a hand is placed on a sheet of paper and the form is delineated with a crayon, the image on the paper will convey a hand, and yet the two-dimensional result will not describe the volume. It is recognizable due to its strength as a symbol. In order to move beyond a symbolic image it is necessary to consider how solid volumes are perceived and how the information gained can be translated into an image that conveys depth or solidity.

Many attempts have been made to equate the human form with simple, geometric or well-known forms: the head, for example, might be likened to a sphere or egg shape with cavities for eye sockets and additions for the nose, ears and neck. The problem with such simplifications is that they are essentially theoretical and in practice do not help with the complexity of drawing. On the other hand, any attempt to convey the contour of a head without first considering its three-dimensional structure will usually result in a two-dimensional image not unlike a child's. It is evident that a balance is required in which the simplification of volume may be acknowledged without over-simplifying the drawing itself.

Once the artist has established the fact that the apparent line around a living form is likely to change and move, he or she can then start to understand how the contour can explain the internal structure, that is, the solid form. The line that appears to separate one object from another in effect defines the point at which the solid volume curves away from view. In the same way, the horizon line at sea is an arbitrary limit — the point at which the actual curvature of the earth prevents a perception of the continuing curve. If the edge or contour of, for example, a globe is suggested by a single unbroken line, the drawing appears to represent a flat object and is therefore not sufficient to explain the volume. It should then be apparent that in order to make an image that does suggest form it will be necessary to reconsider the use of line, or alternatively involve the addition of tone.

By varying the pressure on the pencil, a line of different intensity will result, and by the addition of tone in relation to the effect of light and shade a more substantial indication of volume can be realized. Alternatively the contour may be broken or the directions of lines changed to indicate different planes. In the case of describing a face, certain points around the contour may reveal the overlapping of one form over another. By careful observation it will become apparent that the line that appears to delineate the jaw or cheek actually moves in front of the contour of the neck and what at first appears to be a silhouette is actually a subtle interplay of contours that move backwards and forwards in space, not just two-dimensionally. In attempting to define the volume of the head it is helpful to consider how the pencil point would negotiate different changes in direction if it were to physically move across the actual object in question. Assuming that a head is being considered from a three-quarter view, the apparent contour of the nose would move from below the forehead and then appear to cut across in front of the cheekbone furthest from view. Both Picasso and Mattisse used line with remarkable subtlety, and often indicated the volume of a figure by slight changes in contour without any addition of tone.

Another example of an indication of form by line is evident in the work of Alberto Giacometti (1901 - 66). In many of his early drawings the solid volume is implied by an awareness of the changes of plane that have been encountered while studying the form of an object. The cavity of an eye socket is explained without the cast shadow caused by light on the forehead: the depression in volume is evident by the indication of changes in plane. It is always tempting to underestimate these changes and concentrate on the superficial resemblance of the features. Although the various components of the eye, the iris and pupil, for example, might be clearly visible, a convincing indication of their relative positions cannot be provided if they are not represented resting deep within the eye socket. In portraiture the temptation to emphasize the features must be avoided so that the structure of the head is resolved in its entirety.

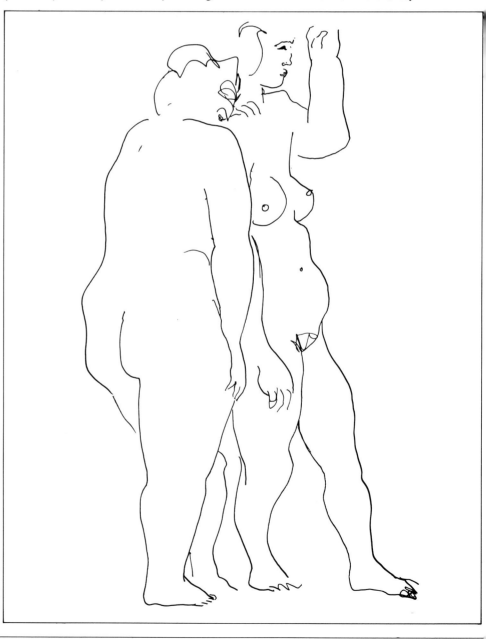

FAR LEFT **Two Nudes** (1956), John Golding (b 1929). This deceptively simple pen and ink drawing is a good example of how line can suggest volume.
LEFT **Caroline**, Alberto Giacometti. Giacometti combined an interest in spatial relationships with a highly personal view of the figure, capturing the isolation of modern life. This painting shows how Giacometti 'drew' with paint, using line and hatching to convey both solid form and space.
ABOVE This pencil drawing shows a high degree of control. The continuous line both evokes form and sets up rhythms.

Perspective

Drawing need not be the result of clinical observation at the expense of expression, and it is worth considering how some artists have come to terms with methods of representing the visual world with some accuracy. The predominance of realism in Western art has hindered an appreciation of drawing as an art in itself; in Eastern cultures there has been less emphasis on the imitative quality of drawing and more appreciation of line and shape. However, developments that have been made with the aim of naturalism were inspired by a growing awareness of perspective. The use of perspective as an aid to figurative drawing reached its peak during the Italian Renaissance. By establishing a fixed viewpoint in relation to a given subject it was realized that an image could be drawn which suggests how an object is perceived in space. This contrasts with the image behaving as a symbol which describes an object's obvious two-dimensional qualities without implying its relative position to the spectator.

If an artist wants to draw a pair of scissors, the outline or silhouette is sufficient to strike a chord in the observer and the image will be instantly recognizable. If, however, the same object is seen from a viewpoint that is not symbolic, the problem of conveying its shape naturalistically is more complex. The same situation occurs when an artist is confronted with a model; the artist must acknowledge the difference between what he knows to be real and what he actually sees.

Before beginning a drawing it may be useful to indicate the eye level and establish an imaginary horizontal plane between the artist's eye and infinity which will dictate the height of the horizon. This level will rise or fall according to the position of the artist, and even though the drawing may proceed in an intuitive manner it is important that this level be related to the position of the model. In theory it is assumed that all parallel horizontal lines converge at a point known as the 'vanishing point'; in practice this may be evident by standing in a street and noticing how the buildings appear to diminish in size the further away they are. The parallel lines of the rooftops and pavements on either side would converge to a single point if the street were long enough. The vanishing point depends for its position on the viewer's eye level, which is a vital consideration in the composition of a picture.

Although it might be assumed that drawing a single figure would not involve perspective, it becomes apparent that the relative position of artist and subject will affect the drawing. If the artist is positioned at the same eye level as the subject and also very close, the subject's head will be seen at eye level but the whole body will be seen from above. If the model is seated on a chair and viewed from a close vantage point, the thighs will be seen from above. If the artist moves further away, the thighs will appear to be

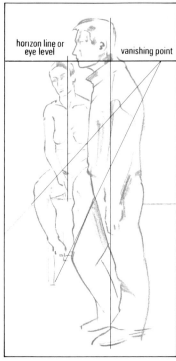

foreshortened and the discrepancy of viewpoint will be less evident.

The complexity of many realist paintings provides a paradoxical result in the realization of this phenomenon. In the work of Jacques-Louis David and Ingres the clarity and detail evident in some portraits suggests that the subject was seen from a close vantage point, and yet the particular application of perspective contradicts this by implying that the whole figure was observed from some distance. More recently Euan Uglow (b 1932) has deliberately emphasized this visual distortion but many artists have compensated for it in an attempt to convey a more acceptable representation of reality.

As with any such theory, its practical application can only be more complicated. A simple

Perspective
Representing three-dimensional form on a flat surface has preoccupied artists and draughtsmen for centuries. The notion of perspective, rediscovered in Western art during the Renaissance, enabled artists to attempt to come to terms with the difference between reality and what they actually saw in front of them. These examples show perspective applied to representations of the human figure. The drawing of the two figures and its schematic outline showing eye-level and vanishing points (**above** and **top right**) illustrate the rigorous planning necessary to express not only the volume of a form in space, but the relationship between the figures. The foreshortened reclining nude (**above right**) shows a figure in a horizontal plane. Because the body is composed of curves and not of straight lines, giving a convincing representation of recession involves keen observation rather than merely a systematic application of fixed rules.

LEFT **Paganini** (1819), Jean Auguste Dominique Ingres. This portrait was drawn during the artist's stay in Rome, where he moved in 1807 after winning a scholarship. It may have been one of the portraits he made – chiefly in pencil – to earn his living after his prize money ran out. Ingres, who had studied in David's studio, went on to become one of the best-known French artists of his day and was firmly identified as an opponent of the new Romantic movement. At the time this portrait was executed, Niccolò Paganini (1782-1840) was on the brink of success as a virtuoso violinist and composer. It is ironic that Ingres should come to portray one of the most influential figures in the rise of romanticism in music. Paganini's life was as extravagant as his aesthetic: he was a womanizer, fond of gambling and noted for acts of extreme generosity. A popular idol in many European capitals, he revolutionized the art of playing the violin. This portrait shows Ingres' sensitive draughtsmanship, yet displays a paradoxical realism. The entire figure is observed in detail, but the twisted pose and recession in space implies that the sitter is viewed from a distance.

acknowledgement of the relative eye levels of both artist and model at least provides a foundation for coming to terms with the representation of three-dimensional bodies on a two-dimensional surface.

Tone

The reason for so far considering drawing in linear terms is not to exclude other approaches but to establish an idea about the nature of perception without attaching too much importance to the effects of light and shade. The addition of tone should not be considered as an embellishment to line drawing, but its use is often the result of the desire to compensate for a lack of three-dimensional volume that probably arises from a misunderstanding of the nature of linear drawing.

A specific problem for the artist in the twentieth century is the acceptance of visual material in photographs. The photographic image is by its very nature reliant on light and shade, however, the tonal quality can provide a false yardstick for the artist and the pitfalls of imitating the apparent naturalism of photographs should be avoided. A photograph of someone's face in strong sunlight can result in an image that is predominantly dark or light and lacking in half-tones. If this effect is copied in a drawing, with dark patches acting as approximations of shadow, the volume of the form, especially in the shaded areas, will be flattened. If a photographic use of tone in a drawing is falsely equated with realism, an understanding of the language of drawing will suffer; 'dark patches' usually amount to a disappointing over-simplification of tonal values. Tone in drawing can in fact be variously used for many purposes.

Before considering examples of tonal drawing it is worth examining its origin which was, interestingly, an extension of linear drawing. The use of tone as 'conceptual shadow' emerged as a

ABOVE **Woman's Head**, Pablo Picasso. This gentle profile study has shallow tonal modelling inside the form and darker tone in the background, which brings the profile forward as if it were a low relief. This use of tone is not intended to give a realistic impression of form, but is an extension of the linear drawing.
RIGHT **Raider with a Cosh**, Eric Kennington (1888-1960).

A combination of rough strokes and smooth blending in this pastel drawing convey different textures as well as volume and depth. The strong light, coming from over the subject's right shoulder, illuminates the side of his face while throwing his body into deep shadow. This strong contrast gives the portrait a striking quality which is almost cinematic in effect.

means of indicating how the boundary of an object disappears from view as it turns around the contour. Byzantine artists made use of this method of indicating volume, and although the result adequately conveyed a form of relief it did not imply a source of light. During the Renaissance the use of tone in relation to an implied light source enabled artists to describe the volume of an object with a degree of realism. As artists became more aware of the optical effects of light they realized that shadow revealed the internal structure of the object and therefore provided an invaluable means of creating a convincing three-dimensional space.

When attempting to draw a figure with a view to considering tonal structure, it is often rewarding to situate the model against a uniformly coloured background. If, for instance, a white wall is chosen and a single light source from one side is used, it will be apparent that where the wall appears to meet the most illuminated side of the face, the wall will seem to be darker than the area that adjoins the shadowed side of the face. By moving the model near to the wall a cast shadow on the wall will be evident and the selection of the most important shadows will reveal the spatial connection of the figure to the background. It will also be evident that the use of a single unbroken contour will impinge on the degree of volume implied when using tone, and that the contour will need to be reconsidered if a convincing representation of volume is to be attained. By closely following the contour it will be evident that it almost disappears at certain points and the edge of the object is indistinguishable from the background.

As the form of an object moves into an area of shadow cast by another object its contour becomes less pronounced and, therefore, if a line of equal intensity describes the light and the dark side of an object the illusion of volume will be hindered. It is important that the tonal structure is considered with the initial structure if the drawing is to have consistency. As the human form is infinitely more complex than a regular geometric solid there can be no easy solution for its realization through drawing. Any attempt to separate by theory the various activities in drawing will not necessarily provide a solution, and the actual experience of drawing combining observation and a sensitive handling of the medium is the best way to learn.

Media

For reasons of convenience the idea of drawing has not so far involved discussion of different techniques and drawing media but it should not simply be assumed that drawing necessitates the use of pencil on paper. The availability of coloured drawing paper and the wide range of drawing implements extend the range of drawing techniques almost infinitely although the fundamental concerns of making a two-dimensional image are similar.

ABOVE **An English Lady**, Hans Holbein. By the late 1520s the Reformation had created major upheavals in Basel: religious paintings were banned and patronage declined. Holbein, who had been primarily a religious painter, was forced to seek work in England. On his first visit he met Sir Thomas More and his family and began work on a group portrait of the family – the first full-length family group depicted in their own home. Holbein's method was to make meticulous drawings from life and subsequently paint from the drawings. Although the group portrait is now lost, the studies Holbein made for this work are still in existence. This fine drawing is thought to be one such study, probably of Margaret Roper, one of More's daughters. It shows Holbein's mastery of line and was executed in black and red chalk, highlighted with white chalk and watercolour. Its delicacy and simplicity place it among Holbein's finest drawings.

Drawing children

Making portraits of children involves a number of particular problems for the artist. Most children do not make ideal sitters; younger ones are usually fidgety and unable to hold a pose for long. While older children are often keen to cooperate, they probably lack the concentration necessary for a prolonged sitting. With patience and a degree of flexibility, however, it is still possible to draw a child from life. Practice making quick sketches will enable the artist to capture fleeting movements: these drawings can later be assembled to provide reference for a more finished work. For a formal pose, it may be possible to alternate short periods of drawing with rest breaks for the child. Even more crucial for children than for older models is the choice of a pose which is not only natural and characteristic, but comfortable as well. Children asleep or concentrating on their play also provide good opportunities for making portraits. If other methods do not work, it is always possible to draw from a photograph, either carefully selected or specially taken for the purpose. In general, pay special attention to the differences in skin texture, proportion and anatomical structure between children and adults and choose a medium that will help to maintain a degree of lightness and vitality.

1. This group portrait is composed in the shape of a triangle, with the poses of the children suggesting a mixture of curiosity and shyness. It is executed in pen and ink, with light smudges to add areas of tone and texture. Since pen and ink does not allow much alteration, the compositional relationships must be carefully considered before beginning to draw. Work from top to bottom to avoid smudging the work.

1

3

4

2. This child was drawn quickly using a 2B pencil on plain white cartridge paper to capture the pose before the boy moved. The hands were emphasized, almost to the point of distortion, to provide a foreground focal point and increase the sense of depth. Pencil marks have been used here not only to delineate the form but also to give overall tone.

3. Another way of introducing areas of tone in a drawing is to apply small patches of paint to counterpoint the line. Here ragged, sketchy lines applied with acrylic paint give an added dimension to the sensitive and careful pencil work of the drawing. The head and cuffs of the dress were emphasized to bring out the quality of the pose.

4. This detail of a drawing of a seated child, made in colored pencil on a page in a sketchbook, shows how a systematic build-up of lines can create the impression of tone and form. This technique is the opposite of using line to imply volume by tracing the contours of a shape. This approach works best using colored pencil.

The common assumption that drawing involves making a dark image on a light surface can in fact be reversed, and the distinction between drawing and painting need not be so obvious. Edgar Degas is renowned for his use of pastels on tinted paper, and in many instances the result achieves the richness of colour and breadth of design that is commonly associated with the use of oil paint and the process of working from dark to light. The art of the twentieth century has resulted in a remarkably diverse attitude to pictorial language which has manifested itself in an equally diverse range of pictorial techniques.

The pencil has always been popular for its accuracy in portraiture. At its best it is simple, quick and effective and can be removed by an eraser if corrections are necessary. The effect of the pencil alters according to the quality of the paper, and a smooth white or off-white paper is often preferred for straightforward effects.

Before graphite was used in pencils, other methods of drawing with a pointed implement were common. During the Renaissance a method of drawing which relied on a confident and disciplined technique using a sharp metal point known as silverpoint was developed. This enabled artists to make delicate and elaborately detailed pictures, carefully drawn because this medium did not allow for any alteration or correction of the initial statement. Evidence of its beauty can be found in the work of Leonardo da Vinci and Albrecht Dürer.

Charcoal may be considered the most primitive drawing implement, yet it provides a more varied range of marks than pencil. Many artists have favoured this medium as a means of exploring the possibilities of tonal relationships. It is usually applied to coarse-grained paper which enables its potential tonal range to be exploited more easily but, as with any medium, the result of trial and error may result in a personal preference for surface quality. Georges Seurat developed many ideas for paintings with charcoal studies of individual figures. He usually preferred a technique that dispensed with any overt use of line, and by establishing a theoretically consistent light source he was able to model each solid form in such a way that the contour combined perfectly with the internal modelling of the form. Chalk has often been used in conjunction with charcoal, especially when off-white or coloured paper is used. A strong feeling of volume can be achieved using mid-toned paper and subsequently adding charcoal for the shadow areas and chalk for the highlights. Many drawings by the Old Masters involve such a tonal range and provided a logical means of preparing to paint in monochrome.

Pastels and crayons are easily available in ready-made form and apart from their own individual properties may be used in conjunction with charcoal and pencil respectively. Pastels are made of ground pigment mixed with a binding

LEFT Detail of **Portrait of Duranty**, Edgar Degas. This portrait of an art critic and novelist shows Degas' preoccupation with draughtsmanship and colouring. Here the two are combined: the basis of the work is distemper painted on unprimed canvas, with pastel overworked to heighten the colour and add to the drawing on the figure itself. The surface pattern of the pastel strokes contrast with the form.

RIGHT **Sleepy Nicole**, Mary Cassatt (1845-1926). An American artist, Cassatt was influenced by the Impressionists, particularly Degas. The rather limited range of subjects in Cassatt's art, however, reflects her status as a woman artist – women were not even permitted to work from clothed male models or venture into the teaching studios. This tender portrait shows her characteristic device of making the figures large in scale, filling and dominating the frame.

medium. The quality of mark can vary considerably due to the ease with which pastels crumble, and in order to keep the pigment on the paper it must be fixed by the application of synthetic resin available commercially in bottles or aerosol cans.

Coloured pencils have become popular quite recently with the precedent set by David Hockney. The obvious advantages of this medium are that it enables the artist to work with the accuracy of pencil and at the same time involve colour. Although pencils are clean, quick and portable, there are certain disadvantages to this medium. The individual colours are available in varying degrees of intensity, but they are generally consistent in terms of softness and hardness. To make a comparison, the ordinary graphite pencil is available in a range from 6H (very hard) to 6B (very soft), and this enables the artist to select the best grade for each particular purpose. Generally speaking, the harder end of the scale is used by technical draughtsmen, and artists normally use the range from B to 6B. The coloured pencil, on the other hand, is generally available in only one grade for each colour and this is roughly equivalent to a B pencil. Consequently it is difficult to cover a large area quickly with dense colour and the drawings often involve a linear technique with areas of tone indicated by blocks of overlapping coloured lines.

Some coloured pencils available are water-soluble and the incorporation of a brush dipped in water, used for blending areas together, can compensate for the linear quality if it is not the desired effect.

The use of drawing ink has always been popular as a medium and can be applied either with a pen or a brush or a combination of both. The quill pen has been associated with ink but there are now many commercial equivalents on sale. A pen holder with a choice of metal nibs provides the means of making a considerable variety of lines and marks, which, by applying diluted ink with a brush may be extended even further.

In the twentieth century, modern technology has resulted in many 'convenience' drawing media. From the ballpoint pen to the fibre-tip pen there are many alternatives to the more traditional approaches. The draughtsman's line pen provides a consistent ink line that will not vary either by pressure or angle of drawing point. It is unsympathetic to the more creative uses of ink and its advantage is mainly of ease.

Choosing a medium

The choice of a particular medium may be influenced either by personal preference or necessity. The distinction between drawing and painting is often based on technique and it is simultaneously assumed that while drawing is primarily concerned with line, painting is concerned with color. This over-simplification becomes meaningless when a number of individual artists are considered, and in some cases the division between painting and drawing is imperceptible.

By considering a few drawings by various artists it will be evident that the particular choice of medium enabled the artist to best convey his particular vision. Ingres used pencil on paper as a convenient way of recording an individual's facial characteristics and at the same time exploring the sinuous contours that could later be used in a painting. Sometimes he continued with a drawing so that it would be complete in itself,

more often the drawing would be used to provide the visual information for a later painting.

When Rembrandt van Rijn drew figures he often incorporated ink line and wash. The consideration of light was paramount and he sacrificed detailed description in favor of a dramatic summary of light and shade. The ease with which Rembrandt implied volume resulted in an expressive use of mark making which can be compared with the fluency of Chinese painting. Nothing could be further removed from the disciplined line of Ingres and yet both artists chose the medium which, apart from any reflection in temperament, best suited the problem.

Edgar Degas was an unusually inventive draftsman. He constantly experimented with combinations of drawing and painting media and sometimes used pastel in conjunction with thinned oil paint over the top of a monotype. His obsession with process is perhaps most evident in the large pastel drawings and yet his recurrent

use of this medium resulted from his attempt to combine the linear quality of Ingres with the spontaneous color of Delacroix. By literally drawing with color he was able to retain the precision of a linear statement and at the same time achieve the rich quality of layered colors. Each successive layer of pastel would be fixed and its application by hatching and cross-hatching would allow the previous colors to show through. Degas had always been fascinated by the technical expertise of the Venetian masters, and by using pastel he sought to find a modern equivalent, creating optical mixtures.

David Hockney has often favored colored pencils for drawing portraits of friends and scenes while traveling. As a result, his choice of medium, whether intentional or not, provides a convenient method of recording accurate visual appearances. His ink portraits are also immediate and unique.

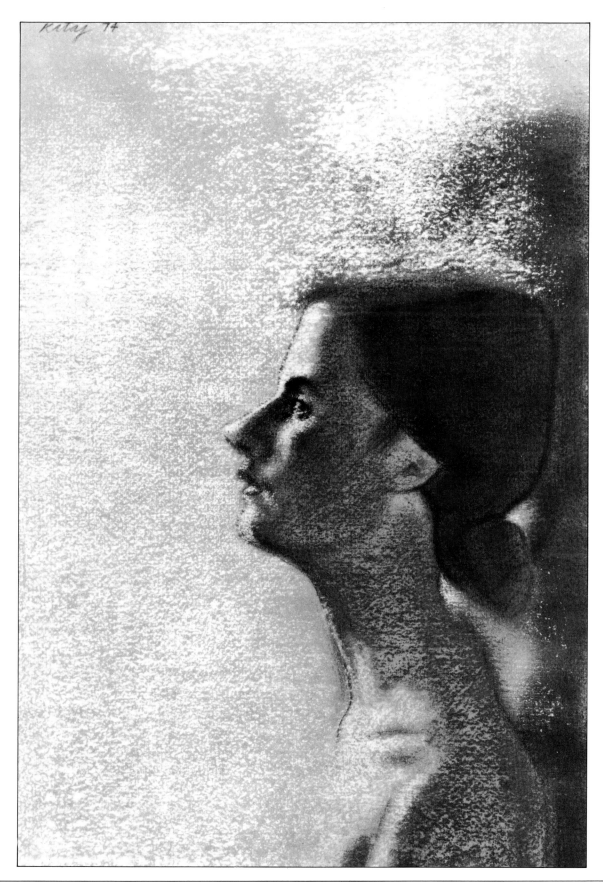

Kitaj 74

FAR LEFT **Christopher Isherwood and Don Bachardy** (1976), David Hockney. In 1969 Hockney made a portrait in acrylic of these two people in the same pose; both this earlier work and the lithograph shown here were inspired by a photograph Hockney took of the couple sitting in their home in Los Angeles. Lithography is an immediate and direct form of printmaking where drawings are made on prepared plates. This example was printed in grey and black on grey handmade paper; the soft, documentary line is characteristic of Hockney's draftsmanship.

LEFT **Study for Miss Brooke**, R.B. Kitaj. Like Hockney, who studied at London's Royal College of Art at much the same time, Kitaj is interested in figurative work. This pastel study shows a characteristic emphasis on contour – the profile of the sitter. Texture is brought out by working into the coarse paper and rubbing back.

Caricature

Caricature is a type of visual shorthand designed to provoke, through exaggeration, some sort of response – recognition mixed with amusement at the very least, although social or political comment is often implied too. Like portraiture, the essential prerequisite is the ability to capture a likeness; the dividing line between portraits and caricatures is not always clearly defined. In general, however, caricaturists isolate and distort the characteristic features of their subjects and are concerned not only with revealing personality but also with the social context. Many artists have shown a fascination with caricature: Leonardo, for example, made many drawings of distorted faces, revealing a preoccupation with oddity and disharmony almost as strong as his interest in perfection and beauty. True portrait caricature emerged in the late sixteenth century but not until the eighteenth century, with the work of James Gillray (1757-1815) and Thomas Rowlandson (1756-1827), was political caricature established as a **genre.** The French caricaturist Honoré Daumier (1810-79) was one of the greatest exponents of this art form. Caricature is dependent to a large extent on line; this linear quality is particularly important for examples designed to be reproduced in newspapers and magazines.

1. **George Bernard Shaw** (1925), Sir Bernard Partridge. This watercolour caricature is a whimsical portrayal of the playwright, the emphasis being placed on the head, face and the aggressive, challenging pose.

2. **Sean Connery** (1974), Michael ffolkes. The humorous magazine **Punch** has featured the work of many cartoonists since its beginnings in the nineteenth century. This cartoon of Sean Connery is an example of the type of caricature which is funny and recognizable, but not savagely satirical.

3. **Salvador Dali** (1980), Richard Cole. Slightly more pointed in its humour, this pen and ink caricature of Dali incorporates Surrealist imagery from the artist's own work to make a striking comment.

4. **Thomas Augustine Arne**, (1710-78), in the style of Francesco Bartolozzi. This coloured etching shows Arne, a composer of music and song for theatres and pleasure gardens, in a humorous pose with his face caricatured. Arne composed the music for 'Rule Britannia'.

5. This modern illustration by Ian Pollock for a book jacket shows the use of watercolour to create a distorted, vaguely ominous figure.

TWO MUSICIANS
pencil on paper

In the absence of live models, the artist may choose to use photographic reference as a substitute. In this case, the artist was inspired simply by the sight of the photograph, and the drawing developed as an intuitive response to the immediacy of the musicians' expressions and pose. They form an interesting composition and their self-conscious, exaggerated stance presupposes an audience. The artist has attempted to recapture the mood; the photograph was also useful as an aid in composing the portrait. Despite the small size of the original, the artist chose to make the figures fill the paper.

This drawing was intended to be preparatory to a later painting, but when finished looked complete and alive in itself. Although the artist is not working from live models, the photograph captures enough mood and clarity of expression for a response to the photograph to be strong and the artist able to copy it with a similar verve and enthusiasm. The initial problem is of scale, the paper being larger than the photograph, but with trial and error the contours of the bodies are established. Proportions are difficult because of the postures (1).

The hair and facial contours of the first figure are filled in using a 2B pencil; this is suitable for both light shading and for the darker blocked-in area of the sunglasses (2). The second face is closely noted from the photograph, and shadows shaping the nose, lips and eyebrows added while the position of the ear is changed with the effect of a slight change in posture. The chin is strengthened with strong lines around the jaw (3).

The postures are well copied, capturing the odd photographic perspective which is reminiscent of the way fairground mirrors lengthen and shorten limbs, and exaggerate one part of a body while making another recede. Hatched shadows across the clothing add detailed volumes to the precise contours, but they are light and sparsely distributed because the contours work well on their own (4).

Textures in the cloth, and small details like collars, a tie, buttons, buckles and turn-ups are added, while the second figure's hand is given precise form. The pencil is used to create stronger, darker lines overall, to blacken the hair and firm up the whole image. An indication of a wall behind the figures gives them a location in space, although it is left deliberately ambiguous to emphasize the fact that they are acting or posing, and do not belong anywhere specifically (5).

5

JANE ON SOFA
charcoal and Conté crayon on paper

When selecting a pose for a portrait drawing it is important to remember that, unless the model is used to posing regularly, the prospect of sitting still for a reasonable length of time may be daunting. The pose should both be comfortable and one which allows the model to maintain a static position.

Aside from providing added interest for the artist, the position of the hand and arm supporting the head assists the model in keeping still for longer than would normally be possible. The back and shoulders are well supported.

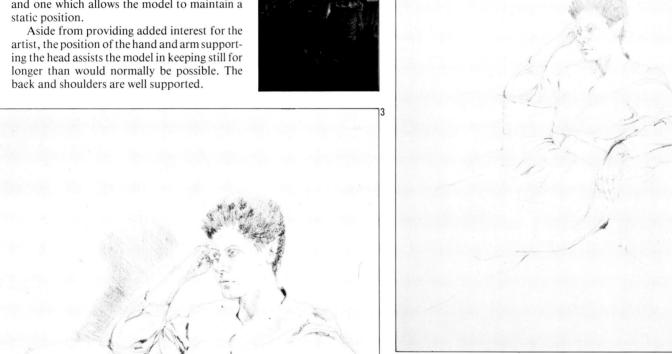

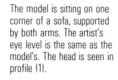

The model is sitting on one corner of a sofa, supported by both arms. The artist's eye level is the same as the model's. The head is seen in profile (1).

The artist chooses to concentrate on the linear format of the figure and not to emphasize the fairly pronounced tonal contrast (2).

By the second stage of the drawing the advantages of the chosen media – Conté crayon and charcoal – become apparent. These permit a greater range of dark tones than would be possible with pencil and help to introduce more depth to the drawing (3). Small areas are emphasized in rich black to give a sense of volume without recourse to the extensive shading or crosshatching that would be necessary with other drawing media such as pen and ink or pencil (4). The drawing is quickly established by darkening areas in turn (5).

The finished drawing shows how the choice of medium can exert a powerful influence over the treatment of the subject. Despite the strong contrast between light and shade that existed in reality, with the left side of the face in almost total shadow, the artist has avoided making tone the main theme of the composition, concentrating instead on rendering the form through the use of simple, delicate charcoal lines. The heavy black shadow on the sofa balances with the way the head is emphasized in the drawing. Both charcoal and Conté crayon produce the type of mark which reveals the grain of the paper; this can be usefully exploited to convey texture, as demonstrated here in the treatment of the hair (6).

OLD WOMAN
pen and ink on paper

If a model is not available, a photograph may prove to be a useful substitute. Although the technical problems of working from photographs are similar to those encountered when working from life, a major difference results from the fact that a photograph is a two-dimensional source of reference. Contour lines are more obvious in photographs and easy to copy, leaving the artist a chance to experiment with technique.

The first step is to establish the basic composition in a linear manner before moving on to concentrate more fully on aspects of the face (1). The eyes provide the artist with a point of focus; their prominence in the early stages of the drawing is compensated for by the addition of darker and more intense shading under the brim of the hat (2). The form of the head is suggested by a gradual build-up of crosshatching, increasing in intensity in the shadow areas. The hands are treated in a similar fashion (3). To increase the range of tonality and bring about a sense of depth, areas of shadow are blocked in completely, notably the shadow to the side of the head (4) and the shadows cast by the hands.

In the final stage of the drawing, the contours have been given more emphasis, using a relatively thick, definite line which contrasts effectively with the spidery marks of crosshatching. There has been no attempt to take the whole drawing to the same degree of completion; areas of the subject's coat are left white and others are indicated by only light areas of tone. From the original photographic source the artist has selected certain aspects of the figure, in this case the face and hands, rather than copying indiscriminately the tonal structure of the photograph. It must always be remembered that photographs can present a misleading view of reality which, if copied, will result in superficiality. Although a photographic image may at first seem to contain sufficient visual information, the artist must be careful to select aspects which convey the structure beneath the surface. In a photograph, the strongly lit or strongly shaded areas of a face, for example, may suggest a very abrupt transition from light to dark. In reality, this change would probably be much more subtle and the artist will need to compensate for this photographic deception (5).

5

JANE IN BLUE SHIRT
pastel on coloured paper

The choice of paper is the first consideration when beginning a drawing and will crucially affect the way that the work proceeds. When making a drawing on white paper, every mark, however dark or light, will be darker than the surface and will consequently imply contours or areas of shade. When working on darker paper, on the other hand, the addition of light marks will imply those areas of the subject that are affected by light.

Toned or coloured paper is often a good choice of surface for a pastel drawing. If the paper is allowed to show through the drawn marks, it will work as a positive part of the drawing.

The model is seated in a fairly upright but comfortable pose, her head resting on one hand. From the artist's viewpoint, some distance away, the head is seen almost in profile, but a small portion of the other side of the face is visible (1 and 2). The drawing begins by establishing the position of the face and hand in white (3). Regular diagonal shading from left to right emphasizes the form of the head (4).

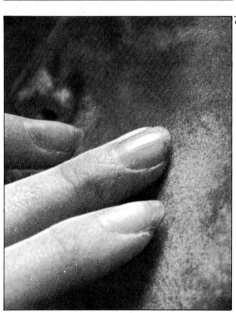

The artist continues to emphasize the dark tonality of the paper by overlaying different colours to build up the areas of the face and hands (5). On closer examination, it is possible to see that the range of marks includes dark strokes as well as the lighter flesh tints. At this stage work is concentrated on the most crucial part of the drawing; and background areas are only sketched (6). Areas on the throat and cheek are smoothed by smudging with the fingertips to create tones which contrast with the more precisely drawn contours. Care is taken not to disturb other parts of the drawing (7).

As the drawing nears completion, more emphasis is placed on the face and hand. The flesh tones become more substantial and a rich surface pattern is built up through the use of a variety of colours (8). The flexibility of pastels as a drawing medium means that they can be used alternately to delineate and shade. Here the bulk of the shoulders is suggested by the simple application of strokes of blue, with gaps left between them to reveal the colour of the paper. At the same time, blue lines also serve to fix the contour of the figure (9). For finer detail, in the shadow areas under the eyes and around the mouth, the artist uses coloured pencil. Rather than applying a range of neutral tones in these areas of shade, green and blue strokes are used which merge with the brown of the paper to create richness and add a sense of volume and depth (10).

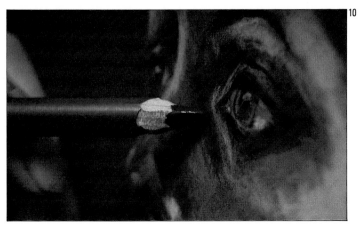

11

Pastel drawing is probably the most substantial way of applying pigment to a surface and the methods of application vary widely. Although it is generally assumed that pastel is best suited to a fairly broad treatment, considerable delicacy and precision of line are possible by taking care while drawing and spraying with fixative at regular intervals. By crosshatching or applying the strokes in different directions, an optical mixture will occur where one colour overlaps another. When viewed at a distance the colours will appear to merge, giving a richness of quality that would not be so apparent with flat areas of colour. In the finished drawing, the brown of the paper also contributes to the sense of depth, cohering the entire image (11).

HELEN
Conté crayon on paper

Many portraitists believe a consideration of the whole structure of the head and face to be vital to a successful rendition of an individual, with features judged only as parts of the whole and incorporated gradually. However, it is possible to reverse this procedure. By drawing the features first, the artist must ensure that they are precisely positioned and the relationships between the features are carefully noted. This method of drawing is only possible if the subject maintains a static pose, and the results are sometimes a little lifeless, but it can be successfully exploited for reasons of facility.

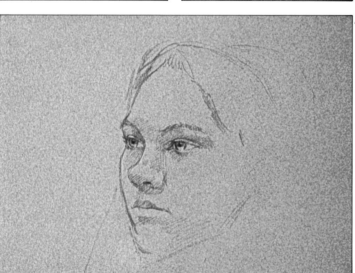

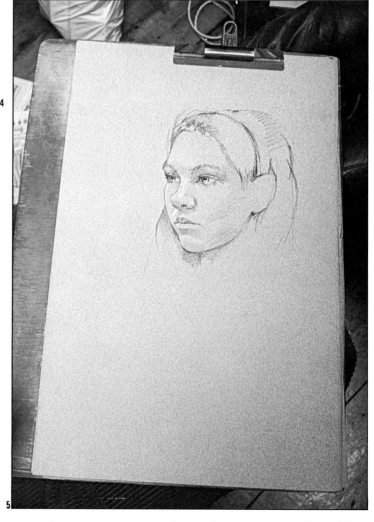

The model is comfortably posed resting against a chair-back. The natural light source is just to her right and slightly above, so her eyes are in shadow (1). The artist positions himself further round, to avoid the straight profile, and works by establishing the line which will describe the side of her face, the brow and her right eye (2), then gradually moves round the face adding precise detail at every stage. The cheek, chin, nose, lips and left eye are drawn in separately, while the artist constantly assesses the proportions and the size of spaces between the drawn marks (3 and 4). Because the paper is already toned, the shadows do not need to be heavily worked while the lights cannot just be left, but need highlighting. White is drawn into areas of the nose and lower cheek to give a greater impression of volume. The back of the head and the left ear are delineated (5).

The detail shows the soft, white Conté crayon being used to describe spots of light (6). Gradually the highlights are built up all over the face, particularly on the curve of the chin, the upper lip, the nose and around the eyes. Light is reflected in a thin line along the rim of the lower eye and softly in the slight hollow above the cheekbone (7). White is also used on the forehead, where it is reflected in a visible line down to the brow. Other streaks of white appear in her hair, over the top of her ear and in a triangle on her neck; the latter form reveals the silhouetted shadow of her chin. Strong contours describe the neck of her shirt and her shoulders (8). Broad, softer lines are used to further describe the movement in the strands of hair and in the shirt. White is used in the background, behind the shoulders, to emphasize the figure on the paper (9).

COLETTE
coloured pencil on paper

When there is limited time to produce a drawing and yet colour is important, coloured pencil is a convenient medium. It enables the artist to dispense with the preparation essential for more complex techniques.

The prime intention here was to establish the face, upper body and hands, with emphasis on the expression. Coloured pencil could not fully convey the richness of the model's clothing, so the drawing presents a visual summary of colour relationships rather than fine differences of texture.

The model is posed at the end of a sofa, her gaze meeting the artist's directly. This type of rapport cannot exist when portraits are made from memory or from a photograph and to bring out the physical immediacy of the pose the artist chose a medium which allows a direct and simple treatment (1).

Using a dark brown coloured pencil the artist begins the drawing by concentrating on the head, gradually moving on to the upper body and hands. With only a limited amount of time, the artist attempts to draw each area quite firmly rather than anticipating subsequent change (2). The face is considered specifically in terms of expression, again bringing out the immediacy of the situation (3). The hair is built up by overlapping masses of dark strokes, allowing white paper to show through in areas affected by light (4). The smooth cartridge paper allows the pencils to slide across the surface (5). Fine hatching brings out the modelling of the face (6).

9

7

8

The use of colour in a coloured pencil drawing is usually related to specific aspects of local colour evident in a quick glance at the subject, such as the bright pattern of the model's dress (7). Although the strength of a pencil drawing usually rests on its linear quality, small areas of tone may be incorporated. The physical difficulty of covering a large surface with pencil usually precludes a dramatic use of tone associated with charcoal or pen and ink work (8). The final stage of the drawing, showing the addition of some background detail, retains a lightness and delicacy (9).

PAINTING THE PORTRAIT

The development of painting techniques

It is no coincidence that the use of oil paint as a medium parallels the development of portraiture in Western painting. It was only when the transparency and elasticity of the medium began to be explored in the Renaissance that the artists could paint skin, eyes and other attributes of the human figure and face with the naturalism that was required to represent individuals. The different ways of applying oil paint during these years of exploration and experimentation were directly related to the simultaneous increase in awareness and understanding of the optical phenomena found in nature.

All painting media have one thing in common: they are comprised of finely ground pigment mixed with some form of binding medium, which might be wax, egg yolk, gum, oil or acrylic, among others. The actual qualities of the paint and the techniques used to apply it are partly dictated by the peculiar properties of each medium.

Early attempts and discoveries

The Greco-Roman funerary portraits found at Fayum in Egypt were painted with coloured wax applied to wooden panels. Although these pictures have proved that encaustic painting is remarkably durable, the problems involved in keeping the wax at a constantly high temperature in order to apply it were generally found inconvenient by the portrait painter. Prior to the Renaissance, many other media were used, the most popular being fresco and tempera.

Although fresco painting does not encroach on the development of portraiture, it seems almost certain that many Italian portrait painters of the fifteenth century had been trained in this medium. Essentially it involved applying water-based paint to a freshly plastered wall surface which, on drying, would bond the pigment with it. Because the plaster had to be wet, it was important that the artist knew exactly how much of a wall could be covered in one session, and the reliance on speed and accuracy

necessitated the use of concise preparatory drawings known as cartoons. Obviously this method was not conducive to life drawing or detailed study of individual faces.

An alternative method to painting directly onto a wall involved making a wooden panel which could be painted in the studio and on completion transported and attached to the wall surface. It was found that when paint was applied to a panel its ability to adhere was greatly improved with the addition of egg yolk as a binding medium. Again the limitations of this technique necessitated the use of a detailed preparatory drawing which enabled the paint to be applied without readjusting the initial design. Because the paint dried so quickly, artists devised methods of applying the paint in short strokes often known as hatching. The result of this method of application enabled artists to paint one colour over another in such a way that the underpainting showed through. It became common practice to paint skin in a green tonality and then overpaint in the more natural flesh colours,

RIGHT This Hellenistic funerary portrait was painted on cypress wood using the encaustic method which has proved remarkably durable, no doubt as desired. The colours and details are still vivid, despite the fact that it was painted in the second century AD. Confident shading and highlights and an imaginative use of limited colours give the portrait a surprising realism.
FAR RIGHT **Enthroned Madonna and Child.** In contrast with the naturalism of Greek art, the later Byzantine works are heavily stylized. When, in AD 311, the Roman Emperor Constantine proclaimed Christianity the official religion of his state, the effect on Western art was profound. Painting was allowed, but only within strict religious bounds as a way of educating the masses. This icon, painted in tempera and gold leaf on a wooden panel, illustrates the effects of the restricting dogma. The faces of the Virgin and her Son are given form by the use of conceptual shadow which denies a specific light source; although foreshortening is used to describe the bodies, the overall effect is more symbolic than realistic.

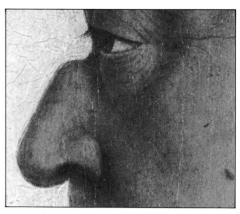

a technique that involved the juxtaposition of muted complementaries.

Artists realized that the value of colour brightness or intensity is determined not just by the positioning of one colour next to another but by the overlapping of one over another. If red pigment is applied to a white surface, it will be greatly altered. If the same red is painted onto its complementary, a green ground, the result will be surprisingly intense. By anticipating the final colour, painters discovered that they could make a preliminary painting in the complementary colour and vastly improve the result. It is not just the colour that causes this enhancing effect: it is also the degree of warmth or coolness. The luminosity of colours and their combinations is evident in normal optical experience particularly in bright sunlight and in the colours of the daylight sky.

Advances in the Renaissance
It is generally assumed that the transition from tempera painting to oil painting was gradual and partly evolved due to the artists' desire to maintain the intensity that coloured pigment attains when it is soaked in water. If coloured chalk dust is mixed with water it immediately takes on a richer appearance but when the colour dries the evaporation of water returns the colour to its former state. In order to maintain the richness, a substance was required that would dry without altering the colour.

Even before van Eyck, artists coated their tempera panels with a form of varnish composed of sandarac dissolved in linseed oil, and before the fifteenth century colours had been mixed with similar kinds of oil for decorative purposes. Because of the heat required in the preparation of such oil it developed a brownish tinge which was obviously unsuitable for covering cool or delicate colours without altering their effect. Whether this factor hindered its use in painting is not known, but varnish was certainly available long before it was adopted as a painting medium by artists. Another problem that arose through experiment was that although the thickened oil made by boiling proved durable and freed the surface from damp, its unmanageably thick

ABOVE **Federico da Montefeltro**, Piero della Francesca. Now considered one of the most important and innovative artists of the **quattrocento**, Piero della Francesca was almost unknown until the last century. A near contemporary of van Eyck, he was working at a time when oil paints were gradually gaining popularity over tempera, and he sometimes used a combination in his paintings. In this portrait, which portrays the nobleman in bold profile and with precision of detail, the tempera paint was laid uniformly and thinly over a wooden panel. Piero used a system of underpainting in complementary colours, and a greenish brown beneath the flesh gives depth to the shadows. The artist assimilated some Florentine ideas on perspective and the organization of space, visible here in the way the paint intensities are diffused for the distanced mountains and in the realistic meandering of the small rivers. It is a powerful portrait, surprisingly alive despite the static pose. ABOVE RIGHT Because of realistic use of lights and shadows, careful modelling is particularly evident in this detail of wrinkled skin around the eye.

TOP LEFT **A Princess of the House of Este**, Pisanello (c 1395 - c 1455). Also known as Antonio Pisano, the artist was a prime exponent of the international Gothic style which was prevalent in some parts of Europe in the early fifteenth century. This portrait, painted in tempera in about 1443, is a good example of the style. Intricately noted butterflies and flowers set into the darkness of the bush provide a mysterious but pretty setting.

ABOVE LEFT **Portrait of a Lady**, Rogier van der Weyden. The costume worn by the subject suggests that this oil portrait can be dated to the 1450s. Painted on a wooden panel, the portrait reveals an air of modesty or perhaps melancholy, the lady's pale face placed formally within the transparent folds of her veiling.

ABOVE **A Man in a Turban**, Jan van Eyck. The extraordinary realism achieved by van Eyck in this and other portraits was mostly due to extensive experimentation and a subsequent mastery of the oil medium. This portrait, thought by some to be of himself and by others to be of his father-in-law, is painted on an oak panel in rich glowing colour using an innovative tonal range. Van Eyck's achievement and his ambition could be summed up in the words, written in semi-Greek lettering on the upper frame of this painting: **Als ich can**, which refers to an old Flemish proverb, 'As I can, but not as I would'.

LEFT **Doge Leonardo Loredano**, Giovanni Bellini. From a talented and innovative family of Venetian artists, which included his father Jacopo, brother Gentile and brother-in-law Mantegna, Giovanni Bellini emerged as an original painter in his own right. His unusual awareness of the changing qualities of light and the way it transforms the objects it touches were his particular domain. Colour and light became for him the most important means of giving expression to his imagination.

In this portrait, painted in 1501, Giovanni's mastery of the oil medium is evident. The simplicity of composition enhances the vivid representation of the Doge's face, while the clear blue background complements the gold of his clothing in which the textures of the embroidery are almost real enough to touch. Light has been subtly exploited to model the face in minute and exact detail; the resulting expression seems humane and understanding despite the stern, controlled aspect.

RIGHT **Pope Julius II**, Raphael. Before he was 20, Raphael, properly called Raffaello Sanzio, visited Florence to study the work of Leonardo da Vinci and Michelangelo; as a result, the powerful figures and the paint quality of his early work bears some resemblances to Michelangelo's. At the age of only 25 his reputation as a great religious artist was confirmed: in 1508, Pope Julius invited him to Rome to paint the frescos for one of the papal rooms in the Vatican. He stayed in Rome until he died aged 37. While in Rome, his commissions were so numerous it became necessary for him to employ assistants and pupils, while he supervised the decoration of ceilings and walls in churches and in the homes of the nobles and intellectuals of Rome. Pope Julius, one of his most important patrons, is painted here in oils with a certain tenderness and great depth of feeling. Hunched in his chair and with downcast eyes, the impression is of an old man dressed in the ill-fitting robes of a religious leader; the slight blurriness of the image enhances the impression of age. The soft, marbled effect of the background throws the strong composition into relief, and the intenser colours describing the trappings of office serve to emphasize the frailty of the man.

consistency did not enable it to be applied delicately. Van Eyck and the Flemish painters are usually credited with the invention of a varnish that allowed colour to maintain the brilliance of wet pigment, and in the course of experimenting the pigment probably dissolved in the varnish; thus oil paint as we know it today gradually evolved.

The mature works of van Eyck, at the beginning of the Renaissance, are separated from Titian's by about 100 years; during this period oil painting developed remarkably. At first the activities of drawing, painting and varnishing were quite separate but eventually the discoveries of versatile oil media enabled artists to treat the three activities as one, and ever since painting has been considered as a separate activity from drawing.

THE IMPROVEMENT OF NATURALISTIC PAINT EFFECTS The early Flemish method of oil painting remained faithfully close to the technical habits of the tempera painters, beginning with a carefully considered drawing on a white ground. Very gradually the shadow areas of the picture would be indicated and the whole design completed by adding dark colours to the light starting colour.

Because of the increased potential of oil paint, artists grew more aware of how colours are perceived in reality. The indication of space in pictures was greatly enhanced by transparent films of colour as this provided a means of describing objects which in reality are distanced by air. The brilliance of colour found in stained glass windows is due to light passing through the glass. If the same glass is seen from the outside the effect is considerably less pronounced. In the same way, Flemish painters grew to realize that if transparent paint were applied to a white gesso panel the colour would retain its luminosity because the light would pass through the colour and reflect back off the white surface.

The use of a white ground meant that, for a painting to exist at all, every addition would be darker by comparison; even the high-key tonality of pale skin would be darker than the light ground. Colour, whether warm or cool, acquires warmth by being thinly applied over a light ground that is allowed to show through. When the reverse happens and a light colour is applied over a dark ground, the effect is cool regardless of the warmth of the applied hue considered in isolation. When artists first used pigment in an oil medium it began to be understood that the optical results were directly related to the optical occurrences in reality, that light and paint behave in similar ways to light and nature.

The Flemish painters certainly used oil painting techniques before the Italians, and much of their success was due to an empirical understanding of the effects. Perhaps not surprisingly, it was only when Leonardo da Vinci applied his scientific knowledge to the problem that the direct link with the actuality of seeing was established. Leonardo forwarded the theory that when distant objects such as mountains appear to be blue in colour, the degree of blueness is directly related to the darkness of the object and the density of the intervening atmosphere. He maintained that this effect could be imitated by placing a colourless or transparent object in front of a dark one, for example positioning a piece of fine muslin over the darkened doorway of a building. The cloth would assume a bluish tinge.

By observing the apparently neutral colour of substances such as smoke, Leonardo also realized that their colour changes according to the colour of the substance directly behind. When smoke is seen against a dark object it appears to be blue in colour, but when it is seen against the sky in daylight it appears to be brown. By considering natural phenomena in this way Leonardo was able to understand how colour and tone could be made to work in a painting and how the overpainting of colours could provide a painterly equivalent for those effects found in reality. If the artist attempts to paint these effects by mixing the apparent colour opaquely, on the palette, the effect will not be the same as when the artist paints, for example, white paint over black allowing the black to show through. When black and white are mixed physically the result is a neutral grey; when white paint is brushed over the top of black the tone may, or may not, be identical but the effect is cool rather than neutral.

In the same way as the history of portraiture may be considered as a progression from the Flemish school to the Italian school and on through the Venetian school, so the development of the technique of oil painting may be considered in three stages. The Italians were generally slow to accept the new technique of oil paint and the painters who did generally followed the precedent set by the Flemish painters. At first, oil was considered to be an extension of tempera and not a medium with its own unique properties. Through his awareness of optics, Leonardo reassessed the situation and radically altered the whole painting procedure to suit his own needs.

One of the main problems encountered by Leonardo lay in the fact that the oil medium used by the Flemish painters was so glossy that it did not allow any reworking after the final layer. Leonardo found that by diluting his oil with spirit of turpentine or petroleum he was able to make his colours clearer, less shiny and more easily workable. Rather than starting a painting with tempera, Leonardo painted the preliminary design in oils, gradually diluting them as the

RIGHT **Knight and Page,** after Giorgione. It is impossible to tell how much of the work often attributed to Giorgione was actually painted by him because he neither signed nor dated his paintings and many of his unfinished pictures were in fact completed by his pupils, one of whom was Titian. Whoever the artist was, this is a striking portrait that owes its originality to an unusual composition and subtle use of tone. Many different shades of black and brown illustrate a mysterious and gloomy light, only relieved by rich streaks of gold, which create a surface pattern of their own. In positions that imply movement, the knight and his young page have lively expressions, perhaps caught in the middle of some action. The interest of the portrait lies in the fact that they are part of a continuing story, but at the same time, the multiple lights and shades describe a uniformity and harmony that only have reference within the picture.

BELOW Detail of **Virgin of the Rocks**, Leonardo da Vinci. Leonardo's technique involved a warm brownish underpainting, followed by the working of blues, purples and cool colours and finishing with warm glazes. This detail illustrates the bluish paint visible through the flesh tones on the Christ child's nose.

RIGHT **Portrait of a Man**, Titian. Painted in a later style in oils on canvas, this is a striking portrait, sometimes thought to be of the young Titian himself. Textures are vividly represented, and the fluid paint handling shows a development.from the opacity of Leonardo's layers.

FAR RIGHT **A Woman and her Child**, Sir Anthony van Dyck. Famous chiefly for his portraits, this Flemish artist treated his subjects with an individual liveliness and confidence. Working a century later than Leonardo, the relaxed pose and happy atmosphere is a sign of an increasing informality in portraiture, balanced by an increasing ease with the medium.

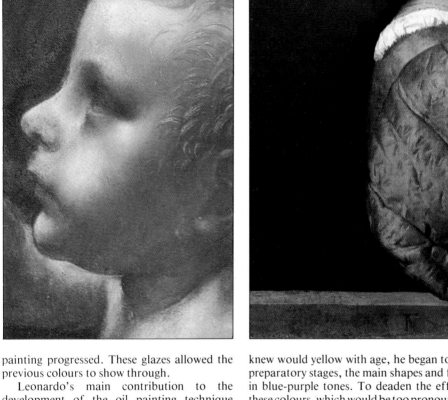

painting progressed. These glazes allowed the previous colours to show through.

Leonardo's main contribution to the development of the oil painting technique resulted in a method of application that allowed for considerable change while painting, rather than the method favoured by the Flemish painters which involved establishing the design with a pointed implement and adding paint afterwards. Leonardo painted the preparatory areas by establishing tones rather than a linear structure — a method that was only worthwhile using semi-transparent paint. Although he succeeded in finding a clearer oil medium than had previously been used, it was still warm in tonality and not perfectly transparent. In order to compensate for this warm glaze, which he always

knew would yellow with age, he began to paint preparatory stages, the main shapes and forms, in blue-purple tones. To deaden the effect of these colours, which would be too pronounced if set on a white priming, he first prepared the panel with a yellowish-brown ground. By following this procedure Leonardo started with a warm, mid-toned ground, painted in cool colours and finished by adding warm colour again. Many of his contemporaries did not follow this method and preferred to work from a linear drawing and from a light ground into dark. The logic behind Leonardo's apparently complex procedure and much of his originality regarding technique was misunderstood.

A problem with Leonardo's theory was that a painting often arrived at a finishing stage before

the complete procedure had taken place, and the final warm glazing, which all the previous applications had been anticipating, was unnecessary. Vasari has stated that this happened to the *Mona Lisa*; although it progressed over a number of years the final glaze of colour was dispensed with and the picture abandoned as unfinished.

Obviously, for a glaze to work it must be darker than the colour to which it is being applied; in other words, the glaze will only provide the richness and depth anticipated if the underpainting or previous glazes have a lighter tonality. They work in the way that stained glass is only bright when the light outside shines through. Leonardo's obsession with creating a strong feeling of volume by emphasizing the darkness

of shadow in the preliminary stages meant that the painting often reached a point where the shadows became unrealistically black, rendering useless any subsequent glazes. Shadows are not usually light in tone but in many instances, the shadow areas of Leonardo's paintings are completely opaque. Many painters after Leonardo tried to remedy this by understating the shadow darkness so that the final glaze of paint would be more effective.

The Venetian painters were quick to exploit the possibilities of oil paint and adopted many of the procedures tried by Leonardo. By subdividing the activity of painting, they were able to consider the initial stages of each picture tonally and only the finishing stages in terms of colour. The use of *chiaroscuro* provided the tonal foundation for their application of countless transparent glazes of colour. Whereas the Flemish paintings were distinct and detailed from early on, and Leonardo brought the early stages of his paintings near to completion monochromatically, the Venetians ignored the details and kept the shape of the painting as loose as possible until much later, to accommodate the subtleties of the final stage.

Because the final glaze relied for its effect on being darker than the preceding one, the Venetian painters deliberately understated the darkness by using reddish-brown rather than purplish-blue. The lightest areas of the painting, usually the skin, would be painted thickly over the mid-toned ground and would be almost white in the lightest part. If there was any clothing or drapery, this would be painted in the light tones of its local colour, often over the top of a priming made in the complementary of the final colour. Similarly, when painting a blue sky, warm cream or brown would first be underpainted to bring out the intensity of the blue before the final glaze. By making the shadows slightly lighter, and by making the lights slightly lighter also, some areas being almost white, the whole picture would develop so that it was perfectly suited to the application of a final glaze of transparent colour, which had the effect of permanently darkening and enriching the picture.

When painting flesh the Venetians were able to dispense with blue because the coolness resulted from the light flesh tones being placed over the darker underpainting. In comparison to Flemish painting, in which the colour of skin often involved the addition of blue, the Venetian effect occured through the optical mixture of pigment. Both techniques resulted in a pearly skin quality often found in reality.

The complete Venetian procedure was similar to the first and only stage of the Flemish technique. Venetian painting involved the use of a range of tones which, if considered as a line, could be seen to begin with dark transparent glazes, progress to semi-opaque mid-tones created using a little white, and end with thick, opaque white paint. This range is based on the way that, in reality, the shadows tend to sink into a scene whereas the highlighted areas are most readily seen. By carefully modulating the paint in this way the result often looks as though it was painted all at once; yet the effect is dependent on the optical mixture of overlaid colour.

This kind of painting procedure was adopted throughout Europe and it was generally considered that dark shadows should be transparent and light areas opaque with half-tones being formed by a mixture of both. In the hands of Rembrandt, Rubens and Velasquez this procedure resulted in powerful yet subtle effects of light and shade. With greater experience gained through studying the early developments in oil painting the artists of the seventeenth century were able to take more liberties with the methods of application, and despite the similar use of the transparent shadows and opaque lights they developed a highly personal visual language.

AN INCREASING SPATIAL AWARENESS When comparing a portrait by van Eyck with one by Velasquez it will be apparent that apart from the technical differences there is a quite different feeling about the space conveyed through the paint. As artists became aware of the relationship between painting procedures and optical experience, certain changes occurred in the way in which the artist observed reality. When van Eyck attempted to paint a portrait, his creative ability combined with a subtle use of oil paint enabled him to recreate in paint a vast array of tactile and visual experiences. Coupled with an awareness of perspective, this technical breakthrough resulted in an art form that has enjoyed popularity because of its apparently imitative nature. However, to consider what actually happens while observing an object that is close at hand is to realize that van Eyck's illusion of reality is in fact paradoxical.

When van Eyck painted a face, the microscopic detail would suggest that he chose to observe his model from a close vantage point. It is fair to assume that, armed with a technique capable of rendering precise surface detail, van Eyck was intent on pushing it to the limits by focusing his attention on each hair and wrinkle in the hope of recreating the complexity of nature in paint. However, when considering the painting as a whole, the result is at odds with his intention. Although some objects are further away from the picture plane than others, they are all treated with the same degree of focus. In *The Marriage of Giovanni Arnolfini and Giovanna Cenami* (1434), all the objects behind and in front of the two figures are painted with the same degree of precision as the two figures. The chandelier, the mirror, the fruit and the sandals are all rendered with a remarkable degree of accuracy. Although each object is presented in its correct spatial position, its accuracy and sharpness would suggest that van Eyck painted each one from a close vantage point and then carefully positioned all of them in their respective positions in the painting.

Although this phenomenon is evident in Italian painting it is more pronounced in Flemish painting because of the tradition of depicting deep space. If an artist is painting a face by sitting very close to the subject, the area around will appear to be out of focus unless attention is deliberately shifted to what is behind the figure. If the same figure is seen from some distance the volume will be less distinct, and there will be less distinction between the figure and its surroundings. Because the flat surface of van Eyck's picture is an object, the spectator can see the face of the man and the chandelier behind quite clearly at the same time. In reality, however, the distance between the two would not allow a viewer to focus on both without either the face or the chandelier being more prominent. Although the composition of the picture is unified in terms of a balanced distribution of masses in space, the fact that each object is observed in isolation results in a disjointedness that is different to the effects achieved by Velasquez and many painters since.

When painters after Leonardo began to use a toned ground, the procedure of painting with transparent shadows and opaque lights ensued. This technical preference resulted from an awareness that objects and people must be affected by light in order to be visible at all. An object in shadow is less distinct and when painted it could be rendered effectively in transparent paint with blurred contours. Leonardo's painting is different from van Eyck's because the shadow areas of a figure or object are pushed back in the picture by transparent glazes. The Venetian painters Giorgione and Titian grasped this phenomenon and also realized that it was essential for the painting to have a convincing pictorial unity. In other words, it should represent a view that would be consistent with the artist looking at the whole scene at once. They retreated from the close vantage point of the Flemish masters in favour of a more distanced view.

The use of a coloured or mid-toned ground for painting emerged through the desire to present the tonal gradations of light and dark by working from the tonal centre outwards, rather than from light to dark. This so-called *chiaroscuro* enabled the artist to unify the picture in terms of light and dark rather than in terms of individual objects. It could not be said that van Eyck was unaware of light, on the contrary his objects would be invisible without it, but he did not consider it as a means of unifying the picture, only as a means of imitating reality. Through Venetian art and on to Velasquez, the idea of light and dark being used as a unifying factor becomes more apparent. In early Velasquez, objects still retain that bulbous reality associated with the close vantage point. The early portraits are so solid, it seems to be possible

The increasing spatial awareness

It is interesting to compare Velasquez' **Merchant of Seville** (1) with van Eyck's marriage portrait (2) when considering how artists' spatial awareness increased between the 1430s and the 1630s. This awareness reflected a growing understanding of the potential of oils and of the way light and colour changes through space. Velasquez distanced the figure behind the merchant and the boy by darkening and blurring his face and his clothing. When compared with the almost tangible, stark realism of the merchant's face (3) and the ceramic jug, these techniques make the background figure less immediate within the picture; however, when noticed, he is equally lively and an integral part of the scene.

The room portrayed by van Eyck, working 200 years earlier, is bathed in a uniform light, and the objects in the background are as distinct as the faces. As can be seen in the detail (4), the chandelier and the mirror are painted as intricately as Arnolfini's face and hat, the only indication of space being the use of perspective. The result, despite the awesome realism of each section of the picture, is dislocated as each object demands equal amounts of the spectator's attention. By comparison with Velasquez' portrait, which gives an indication of a story, the marriage portrait is a simple statement of fact; the objects and people, observed in isolation, are not coherent enough to imply that the figures ever lived, or grew old.

BELOW **Don Andres del Peral**, Goya. The Spanish artist, painting at the turn of the nineteenth century, was profoundly influenced by Caravaggio and Velasquez. RIGHT **Madame Moitessier Seated**, Ingres. This portrait, finished in 1856, displays the wealth of the subject, a member of the French bourgeoisie during the Second Empire. The blatant expense of the gown and luxury of the setting are represented in minute detail. FAR RIGHT **Elena Carafa**, Edgar Degas. Painted 17 years later than **Madame Moitessier Seated**, this portrait displays different artistic aims. The colours, patterns and textures are briefly described and epitomize Degas' ability to sum up atmospheres economically.

to reach out and tap the skulls. With experience, Velasquez played down such obvious illusion and by distancing his vision he sought to describe not just the faces and objects but the distances in between.

Although the difference between van Eyck and Velasquez may not seem important, the development from one to the other has left its indelible mark on the history of Western art. It is sometimes assumed that when an artist is composing a painting, the physical organization of objects and people in space is the main problem. When the portrait painter is confronted by a subject, the position of the figure in relation to any other objects in the room should, perhaps, be considered. Van Eyck, for example, positioned objects in the marriage portrait with considerable care in order to achieve some kind of balance. The equal distribution of possessions around the room accords with the overall symmetry of the design. The spatial organization of such a painting results in a distinct difference between foreground and background, and while the figures and the objects may be considered as positive, the space around and behind may be considered as negative.

By comparison, in *Las Meninas*, a work by Velasquez, there is less emphasis on such a

distinction, and foreground and background are unified as the result of a different approach. When Velasquez prepared the composition, rather than move the objects he moved his own position; by forgetting about the individual characteristics of objects he considered the pictorial organization of his subject in terms of lines and shapes. Velasquez distanced himself from the subject and attempted to recreate in paint a momentary glimpse of reality. Although each area of the painting would have required individual attention during the physical act of painting, it would have been conceived as part of the whole. In this respect Velasquez directed

his attention to the distribution of light and dark rather than the distribution of people and objects.

Further analysis of light and form

The Impressionist painters were quick to identify with the apparent casualness of Velasquez' technique but they were not enamoured with the use of *chiaroscuro*. The idea of considering light in terms of dark and light amounted to a kind of visual heresy. The colours in the spectrum produce white light so it was assumed that light in a painting could be created by the juxtaposition of colours rather than tones. The disintegration of

Late nineteenth-century portraits

1. **Captain Frederick Burnaby,** James Tissot (1836 - 1902). This nonchalant pose epitomizes the ease and gallantry of a popularized nineteenth-century ideal: Captain Burnaby was a hero of his time. Reputed to be the strongest man in the British Army, he died from a spear wound in Khartoum in 1885.

2. **Cha-u-Kao, the Female Clown,** Henri de Toulouse-Lautrec (1864 - 1901). Breaking ground with his unusual viewpoints and compositions, Toulouse-Lautrec represented Parisian low-life in his drawings, paintings and lithographs with enormous vigour and sympathy.

3. **Study for Madame Pierre Gautreau,** John Singer Sargent (1856 - 1925). The finished work for which this is a study caused a scandal when it was first exhibited in the Salon of 1884 because of the daring pose. The black dress is treated almost as a negative space, throwing the white flesh into relief, as if it were a portrait bust placed on a column.

4. **Self-portrait**, Vincent
van Gogh. The artist's many
hundreds of pictures had a
strong influence on abstract
painters because his aim
was not to use colours to
reproduce visual
appearances but to express,
and cause, emotion. He
suffered, particularly towards
the end of his life, from
depressions and
hallucinations; the thick,
swirling paint quality of this
self-portrait expresses this
mental anguish. Colours not
usually associated with flesh
are included, not just to
complement the skin tones
but as an integral part of the
total impression.
5. **Woman in Black**, Mary
Cassatt. This portrait, painted
c 1882, is composed to
boldly fill the canvas. The
paint is loosely and thinly
applied in large brushstrokes,
but the outline of the dress
is solid. The face and hands
are well observed and
painted with more opaque
pinks and whites. To soften
the outlines of the fingers,
the paint was dragged, when
wet, with a clean, dry brush.
The result is lively and
impressionistic.

the boundaries between foreground and background continued with the result that objects were deprived of their tangible volume and described in terms of light flickering across their surfaces. Although the liberation of colour enabled the artist to dispense with the more laborious academic procedures involved in making paintings, it imposed certain limitations in terms of technique. By rejecting the tonal ground in favour of a white one, the Impressionist painters wanted to achieve luminosity and freshness, but this was at the expense of a richness and subtlety. In the same way that Velasquez translated the individual characteris-

tics of a person or object into areas of tonal relationships, so the Impressionists translated and dissolved that tonal structure into areas of colour.

When confronted with a figure, the Impressionist painter would consider the shadow area of the face as a series of patches of colour and reflected lights. The apparent blueness of a shadow would be simplified as a blue shape; if this shadow occurred on the side of the nose then it would be considered with the same impartiality as the shadow on a vase. The fact that it was part of the nose would be almost irrelevant, and the main concern of the painter would be to

forfeit anatomical integrity in favour of the pictorial organization of colour. The problems of reconciling human appearance and emphatic colour perhaps accounts for the rift that occurred between those artists intent on exploring light and colour and those intent on describing human appearance. The work of Edgar Degas provides the visual evidence of this dilemma. His transition from the early tonal portraits to the monumental figure studies of his maturity shows how his predelection for describing the particular characteristics of his individual sitters gave way to the more universal image of his later nude figures.

ABOVE **Self-portrait**, Gwen John (1876 - 1939). A woman of independence and determination, the British artist Gwen John spent most of her life almost as a recluse and in great poverty, despite much hard work. The pose and mood of this self-portrait, painted in her mid-20s, exemplifies that of many of her portraits of others – pensive figures viewed frankly in half-length poses. Her subtle use of oils displays a control over the medium; she exploited many shades of similar colours, mostly browns and rusts, to create a warmth and uniformity.

RIGHT **Interior near Paddington 1951**, Lucian Freud. The realism of this portrait lies in the meticulous observation of the room and the view through the window. However, this technique also creates confusion: like van Eyck, Freud disregards the way objects further away lose their clarity, and as a result there is an underlying sense of unreality. This, combined with the unrelenting brownness and the unspecific title, attempts to deny the individuality of the figure, who nevertheless possesses a unique face.

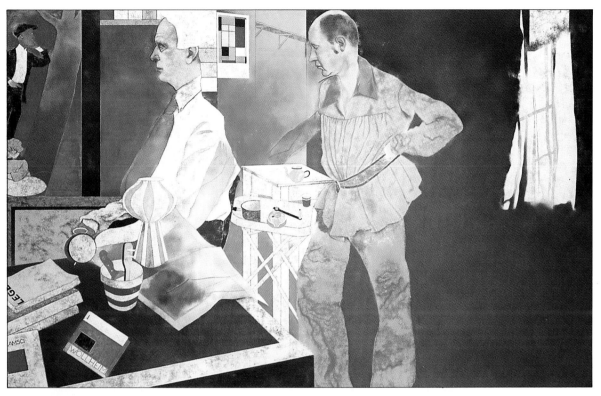

LEFT **From London (James Joll and John Golding)**, R.B. Kitaj. This double portrait, finished in 1976, gives a lively impression of the two men and their room with small details adding particular interest. However, unusual techniques create a disconnected vision. Bright colours are used for their inherent qualities and not because they imitate reality. BELOW **Melanie and Me Swimming**, Michael Andrews (b 1928). Fully evocative of a watery scene, the clear colours and sharp outlines of this work are painted in acrylics on canvas. The blackness of the water seems transparent, partly by inference because the man's lower limbs are distorted through the ripples. The skin pinks and the whites of the splashes are shaped to give a strong sense of movement, while the mutual trust of the two is evident in the balance between them.

Degas' attitude to painting portraits resulted from an empirical understanding of the work of the Old Masters. He was obsessed with trying to recreate the same subtlety that he admired in Venetian painting and yet ironically ignored all documentary evidence on the subject of technique and also the recent scientific experiments in the chemistry of painting. The problem with basing technical knowledge on direct observation of completed paintings arises because the surface denies any investigation of the preparatory stages. Although there is considerable written information relating to technical procedure, it cannot be assumed that painters did not deviate from accepted conventions, and certainly technical advances involved at least a partial rejection of what had gone before. The would-be portrait painter of the 1980s is faced with an abundance of technical choices and historical precedents.

Painters have found more scope in the description of human appearance than in any other visual phenomena. The twentieth century has seen the portrait as a subject for dissection; Picasso delighted in rearranging the human face in a way that his predecessors would have found incomprehensible. In an effort to keep in step with the twentieth-century style, artists have subjected human appearance to a vast array of pictorial surgery, removing and isolating features and presenting different views of the same person in one pictorially unified image. More recently some artists have tried to reconcile twentieth-century ideas with the practices of the masters of the preceding centuries.

Colour theories

During this century there has been a pronounced interest in the use of pure colour, and consequently an abundance of information relating to its theory. In many instances the use of colour is considered in relation to the colour wheel and the respective roles of primary and secondary colours. The theories themselves have existed for centuries, independent of verbal formulation. It is not necessary for artists to research the theories scientifically, but before starting to paint, it is worth understanding basic colour relationships. The practical application of this understanding is, however, limited by the fact that painting does not always involve uncomplicated colour combinations. A further problem is the fact that the very nature of paint necessitates some consideration of the colour value of the prepared surface of the panel, paper or canvas.

The colour wheel is a useful, quick guide to understanding simple colour theories. The artist's three primary colours — red, yellow and blue — can be mixed in pairs to create three secondary colours —orange,green and indigo. The wheel illustrates these six hues merging to form a complete circle, each colour being opposite its complementary. Red is opposite green,yellow opposite indigo and blue opposite orange. The complementary colours are mutually enhancing and have been juxtaposed in paintings to create extra intensity or emphasis throughout the centuries. They may also be painted in layers to give depth. For example, a warm cream or brown colour may be painted beneath a blue sky and the result be close to the reality it attempts to represent. Similarly, a pink provides the muted complementary to green. The complementaries do not need to be of equal intensity to provide the required effect.

Any colour can be varied in tone and in intensity. The tone of a colour depends on its lightness or darkness against an imagined scale ranging from white to black. The intensity or chroma of a colour depends on how much colour there seems to be when, for example, an object is seen through the atmosphere, or when pigment is mixed in water or some other transparent medium. For instance, the local green colour of a tree will gain a bluish tinge at a distance; similarly, a pinch of powdered pure red pigment, although very intense and bright at close range, would become semi-transparent and pale when diluted with water.

Such definitions and theories lead to a consideration of a particular quality of colour as an idea and not in relation to its practical application. The artist who is concerned to reproduce exact colours must take care when purchasing pigments, because these theories only work if the pigments are pure. Artists' colours, particularly cheap ones, are often impure and, when mixed with others, may produced unexpected or slightly muddied results.

Presuming that the paint is reasonably pure and can be controlled, any one colour is capable of taking on different aspects depending on how it is placed in relation to others. In pre-Renaissance paintings, when the number of available pigments was severely limited, one colour might have been given two or three different values by careful placing or layering. As well as being aware of the value of complementaries, it is vital to notice the warmth or coolness of colours. Orange and red are usually considered to be warm in comparison with a light blue, for example, but such generalizations can easily be rendered meaningless by the actual activity of one particular shade next to or over another. By placing a warm colour such as red transparently over a blue, the cool colour might be affected in such a way that it appears to be warm. The greatest advantage of oil paint is its natural transparency which enables artists to render these colour differences optically rather than just physically by mixing.

Media

The boundaries of portraiture are almost indefinable, and the methods and techniques by which they may be created can no longer be defined in the rigorous terms of previous centuries. The fact that oil paint dominates the history of portraiture does not preclude the use of other, more immediate methods of painting.

Experiments in watercolours and gouache

Watercolour and water-based gouache paints are suitable for quick colour studies and the limitations of such techniques in portraiture are compensated by their advantages. The importance attached to oil paint is mostly due to its imitative abilities. It is not possible to paint skin with such accuracy in watercolours but their transparency is suited to experiment, and to coming to terms with paint generally. An awareness of the fluid nature of handling will prepare the artist for the more daunting prospect of painting in oils or acrylics. The opaque quality of gouache, which has white added, is useful for practising working up to the lights, with pure watercolour used for shadows and mid-tones.

Another advantage to experimenting with water-based paints is the relatively inexpensive support that is required for the purpose. Although watercolour paper is preferable, any fairly substantial paper will suffice and this may be pinned to a board or soaked in water and attached to the board with lengths of gum strip around each edge. Once the paper is glued to the board in this way it will shrink when dry and be stretched taut enough to absorb the wet pigment without the surface wrinkling.

The uses of acrylics

The most significant development in recent pictorial techniques is the invention of acrylic paint. The properties of this versatile medium

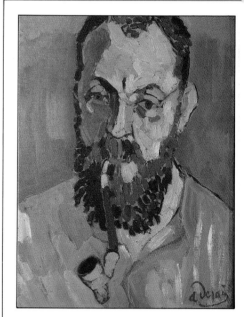

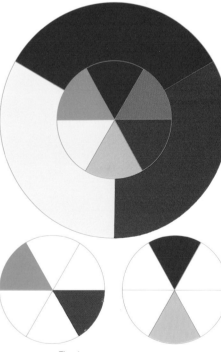

ABOVE AND RIGHT The three primary colours – blue, yellow and red – are shown on the outside of this wheel, and are combined with the secondaries – green, indigo and orange – in the centre wheel. Secondaries are created by mixing the two surrounding primaries in each case. Complementary colours are those from opposite sides on the wheel: blue and orange, yellow and indigo, red and green are the pairs which complement and enhance each other when placed in juxtaposition.

FAR LEFT **Portrait of Matisse,** André Derain (1880 1954). Derain was a member of the Fauve group of artists which included Matisse, Rouault (1871 -1958) and Vlaminck (1876 -1958). They were all interested in the use of pure colour to express emotion; sometimes they used it arbitrarily or for decorative effects, but otherwise to create volume, as Cézanne and van Gogh had done before. Here, Derain exploited intense colours to mould the shape of Matisse' face seen in a strong light.
LEFT This detail shows how the artist worked **alla prima**, applying all the paint in the same stage, working 'wet into wet' on the beige ground which is left bare in places. The thick paint and obvious brushstrokes provide a heavily textured result which matches the boldness of the colour. Reds are set against dark greens, and blues against oranges.

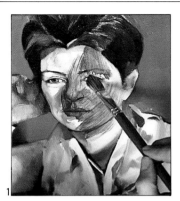

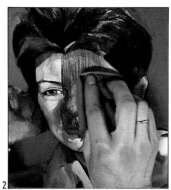

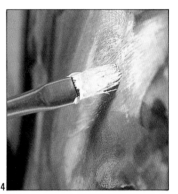

Applying glazes and overpainting
The series of five details illustrates how oil glazes can be applied. The layer to be worked over is light in colour so that light will reflect off it through successive layers. A thin brown is brushed over the face area, so that the dry underpainting still shows through (1), then a cloth is used to spread the paint evenly and to wipe off the excess (2). Highlights are left white around the eye (3). Using a similar technique on another portrait, the artist overpaints thicker white highlights onto the brown glaze (4). Having sandpapered the background, the artist paints a blue-grey glaze for a changed effect (5). The palette includes a range of reds and browns mixed from vermilion, cadmium yellow and cobalt blue (6).

are often underestimated and they possess many of the characteristics of both oil and water-colour. Unlike both, acrylic paint dries in distinct layers and is therefore well suited for glazing. With watercolour, the subsequent additions of paint to the same area of paper dissolve and mix with the preceding ones, except at the edges of dry areas. The problem in oil painting is that the length of time necessary for an area to dry conditions any further applications of paint to the same area. Acrylic paint's most distinctive advantage is its ability to dry quickly and permanently. This allows the artist considerable freedom and allows constant changes to occur throughout the procedure. Acrylics may be used on paper, cardboard, hardboard and canvas with equal success. When used on paper the properties of acrylic are similar to those of other water-based paints; when they are used on canvas their properties are not dissimilar to those of oil paints.

One of the most interesting and useful qualities of acrylic paint is that it can be employed in conjunction with, or instead of, oils. Rather than working directly into a white ground with oil paint, the initial stages of the work may be indicated with washes of acrylics. Because of their quick-drying qualities, they are suitable for spontaneously and creatively establishing the main forms of a portrait.

Often the most daunting yet enjoyable aspect of painting involves coming to terms with the untouched surface of the canvas. For the

painting to progress, it is necessary to cover the areas of white primer. By using acrylic paint the whole surface may be covered with a thin wash of colour, or alternatively different coloured washes for different parts of the painting. This may be particularly helpful when the subject is situated against a light-coloured surface such as an interior wall. If the artist attempts to paint something of light tonality onto a white ground, the colour may appear to be lifeless. By first painting the area in a mid-tone or a neutral grey, the final colour will appear to have more body. By using acrylic paint for this purpose the painting may involve several layers of quickly applied colour which, if they were in oil paint, would take a considerable time to dry. It should be remembered that it is not possible to paint with acrylics over oils.

The choice of technique is obviously a personal matter and may depend on the time available or the size of the painting in question. Using acrylic the portrait painter will be able to paint the initial washes of transparent colour in the same sitting as the oil paint. This kind of technique is considered by many to be indispensable when appoaching the difficulties of painting human skin. Although some painters since the time of the Impressionists have favoured the technique involving the direct application of opaque paint onto a white surface, this is not suited to conveying the subtlety of human skin. Prior to the nineteenth century, painters realized that fair skin often changes in colour depending

on reflected light and the colour of the surrounding objects. It was also realized that the tone of the skin appears to be cooler in some parts of the body, especially where the bone structure is more visible. By using a cool underpainting of blues and greens, thinly applied flesh tones will give this impression; the skin at certain points on the forehead, for instance, can be made to look thinner than the skin of other parts of the body.

Oils
If the artist chooses to use oil paints, any preparatory application of paint, unless left to dry, will mix physically with the subsequent paint applications. Oil paint is a remarkably versatile and flexible medium, and many artists have capitalized on its slow-drying quality by moving the paint about on the surface for the duration of the painting. The technique of *alla prima*, or painting the complete picture in full colour in one session, has gained popularity since the nineteenth century. This usually involves working directly onto a ground with wet paint and adding colour without gaps for drying. The spontaneity of such an approach can be more immediately creative, and painters who prefer this method rarely resort to any preparatory stages on the canvas itself. However, the activity of painting 'wet into wet' can sometimes lead to an uncomfortable build-up of paint which, because of its opacity, renders the ground colour or priming useless. The physical thickness of the paint itself can clog the

surface to such a degree that further application is hindered, and in this situation it is sometimes as well to leave the painting alone or remedy the situation by scraping off the excess paint.

Occasionally, however, this kind of necessity provides interesting results that could not otherwise have been anticipated. A close examination of some of Degas' paintings reveals that he used this kind of accidental effect to advantage. His creative nature was often not satisfied by the results of orthodox painting procedures and sometimes while painting a figure he would feel that the head was being overpainted. He would then wipe away the excess paint and in the course of so doing reveal a more interesting paint quality closer to his intentions. Rather than wiping out the image completely, Degas would keep the remaining thin paint or stain which suggested a particular quality or mood that the more logical paint application hindered. Although he was interested in traditional methods of oil painting, his personal technique did not rely on such means of describing visual appearance. Even a cursory glimpse at his paintings reveals quite different techniques varying from thin transparent washes to thick opaque paint. Sometimes he applied the paint in short strokes or hatchings, sometimes in carefully modulated areas. In some parts of the painting the grain or tooth of the canvas would be evident and yet an adjoining area would reveal a history of colour changes and different densities of paint application.

SURFACES Before any painting can begin, the artist must first select the medium and then prepare the painting surface and the palette. If acrylic or oil is accepted, then it will be preferable to prepare a canvas or a panel. Different kinds of wood may be used for panels but the cheapest and most convenient is hardboard. It is available in large sizes; these provide expansive work surfaces without needing to join the pieces together. First of all, it is preferable to wipe the hardboard surface free from grease

ABOVE **Woman Bathing in a Stream**, Rembrandt van Rijn. The woman's skin is painted quite thickly in the highlights and with great tonal subtlety to give an impression of solid flesh in a diffused light.
ABOVE RIGHT Detail of **Woman with Rosary**, Paul Cézanne. Using strong brushstrokes to delineate contours, Cézanne involved a mass of different colours and tones in thinner paint to achieve the look of flesh.

RIGHT Detail of **Two Ladies of the Lake Family**, Sir Peter Lely. Blended tones and precise attention to detail are exploited to achieve the smoothness of flesh. Green underpainting and the weave of the canvas show through in shadows while the highlights on the cheeks, nose and earring display fine modelling. Thin strands of hair add to the finesse.

with petrol or denatured alcohol and then, if a gesso ground is required, the panel should be sized on both sides with a preparation of rabbit-skin glue to prevent warping. The glue may be obtained from an artists' suppliers, or an equivalent from household decorators may be used called anti-fungal decorating size. The granules are dissolved in water until soluble and then, with the addition of more water, heated gently in a double pan. Although the size should not be boiled, it should be applied to the panel while it is still hot. The same preparation may be used on canvas.

When the glue is dry a further preparation made from one part glue size solution, one part whiting (made from French chalk or precipitated chalk) and one part zinc oxide powder is applied while it is still warm. On drying, further coats may be applied. It is always preferable to use the smooth side of hardboard which may be roughened slightly with some fine sandpaper to give the primers something to grip to, and several thin coats are preferable to a thick coat.

If a canvas support is required it will be necessary to stretch the canvas over a wooden frame known as a stretcher. These may be bought ready-prepared from art shops or alternatively made especially for the purpose. The obvious expense of buying commercially prepared stretchers has resulted in many artists preparing their own. Most art students make them with lengths of 3 x 1 in (8 x 3 cm) wood; each side of the stretcher is lap-jointed or mitred and then glued and screwed. If the stretcher is to be larger than 3ft (1m) square, it may be necessary to add lap-jointed cross-members for extra support. It must be remembered that once the canvas has been stretched and sized, it will shrink and exert considerable stress on the stretcher, while it is drying. Unless the wood is sufficiently supported or strengthened it will warp; the larger the painting the more cross-members will be required. In a stretcher of moderate size, for example about 5 x 4ft (1.5 x 1.2m), one cross-member will probably suffice.

The quality of different canvases varies considerably. They are usually available in materials such as cotton, linen, hemp and hessian, and also in different weights. The important thing is that the weave is close and free of knots and flaws. The easiest method of stretching canvas is to use a staple gun. Although tacks were originally used, the ease with which staples may be applied makes this concession to the twentieth century an invaluable time-saver. Roughly staple the canvas in its approximate place with the weave parallel to the sides, using one or two staples at each corner. Continuing from the centre of one of the longest sides and on the side directly opposite, apply the staples either to the back of the stretcher or the outside edge. Moving to one of the shorter sides and then to its opposite, add a few more staples. When each side is firmly attached by three or four staples in the

RIGHT A particular canvas may be chosen for the size of its weave, for its roughness or smoothness, for its imperviousness or for the way it absorbs the paint. Canvases are made from linen, cotton, a linen-cotton mix and hessian. Unbleached calico is a cheap cotton weave (1). A good quality cotton canvas feels as fine as linen when it is well primed (2). Hessian is coarse and needs effective priming if a smooth effect is required (3). Linen (4 and 5) is generally available in several sizes of weave, the most expensive being closely woven. Linen primed with acrylic is multi-purpose (6).

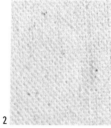

centre, check that the weave has remained parallel to the sides of the stretcher. Work out from the centre of each side by adding half a dozen staples or so and then turning the stretcher around so that each side progresses evenly to the corners. By working in this way a check may be kept on the tautness of the canvas.

The next step it to select a ground before priming the support. If an oil-based primer is selected, then a coating of rabbit-skin glue will be essential in order to seal the canvas and make it non-absorbent. There are many recipes available for making grounds but they are not all for use on canvas. Canvas continues to be the most popular painting surface because of its flexibility, but this advantage renders certain preparations useless. During the course of painting, the canvas will be continually stretching and springing back into shape. Atmospheric conditions will also affect the surface by causing it to expand and contract, and so a ground will be

ABOVE LEFT Detail of **Te Reroia**, Paul Gauguin: Taken from one of his Tahitian paintings, this detail shows a woman's eye which was painted on rough, unprimed hessian. The coarseness of the canvas expresses a primitive quality in the painting, which matches the content of much of his work. Painting on such a canvas was not, however, so much a matter of choice as necessity, as he lived in conditions of poverty in the South Sea Islands. Being unprimed, the canvas absorbed the paint as it was applied, with the result that the colours seem dull and muted, an effect which is emphasized by the

darkness of the hessian.
ABOVE RIGHT Detail of **Mr and Mrs Clark and Percy**, David Hockney. Compared with Gauguin's canvas, Hockney's is finely woven.
The plain weave cotton duck canvas, primed with a thin, white acrylic gesso, is just visible beneath the acrylic overpainting, which is applied thickly in the highlights and also to emphasize the effects of mascara. Hockney used the fine canvas for a deliberately smooth total effect in this painting. Even on the finest support, however, the threads which are woven over the others will catch the paint while a brush will pass over the hollows.

LEFT **Portrait of Jean Muir** (1979), Anthony Green (b 1939). The artist has exploited the unlimited potential of shapes in much of his work. The resulting picture makes the spectator feel privileged with a private view into a section of the subject's house.

prefer not to use black paint, white paint will certainly be essential in larger quantities than any other colour. A fairly strong yellow will be useful, either cadmium yellow or cadmium yellow pale; also a yellow ochre and possibly raw umber. Various kinds of red pigment are easily available, and again the choice is based on personal preference. A strong crimson is sometimes selected but greater quantities of vermilion, light red or Indian red may be more useful. Added to this will be a blue, either cobalt or ultramarine, and also a green, perhaps terre verte.

Joshua Reynolds advocated the use of a limited palette of white, black, Indian red, and raw umber. Although the omission of blue may seem surprising, the colours chosen provided three muted primary colours which through optical mixing would provide the warmth and coolness of their primary equivalents. The brightness of colour is not necessarily due to its purity of hue but to the way it is related with the other colours in the picture. Edgar Degas once expressed his contempt for the seemingly arbitrary excesses of some of his Impressionist contemporaries in their use of bright colour. He remarked that he could paint a picture that would appear to be full of colour using only varying shades of mud-coloured paint because they are both warm and cool.

Paints are available in loose pigment form or otherwise commercially prepared in tins or tubes. In this form they are packaged in different quanties and also in different strengths depending on whether they are extended, as in 'students' colours', or concentrated, as in 'artists' colours'.

As well as plenty of newspaper and rags for wiping brushes, it will be also necessary to acquire some jars for cleaning brushes and containing the painting medium. Pure turpentine is essential for mixing colour — it binds the pigment but has the advantage of being much thinner than oil — and turpentine substitute or white spirit will be needed for cleaning brushes during the process of painting. After each painting session the jars of turpentine may be left, and the next day the pigment will have settled, allowing the clear turps to be poured off and used again. Purified linseed oil may be used as a mixing medium in conjunction with a siccative or drying agent, but this must be added sparingly as cracking may occur if the drying is accelerated.

Many kinds of painting media are commercially available for use in oil painting. They include copal oil medium of different grades, wax medium, stand oil, retouching varnish and many other equivalents sold under different trade names. For oil or acrylic painting a good selection of bristle brushes is needed. The selection may be extended with the addition of decorators' brushes which, although coarse in quality, are excellent for covering large areas of the painting. Palette knives may be used not only for mixing but as an alternative to the brush.

required that is both non-absorbent but also durable and flexible. This immediately eliminates many, if not all household decorators' preparations and also the gesso grounds which are too brittle to bear constant movement. A simple homemade ground consisting of flake white, linseed oil and genuine turpentine provides an adequate base for oil painting, but to save time oil-based primers are also available ready-made from artists' suppliers. They are made especially for the purpose and because they are available in tins may be stored and used without waste. Alternatively, an acrylic-based primer is commercially available and equally suitable for oil and acrylic painting. If this is preferred it will not be necessary to size the canvas as it will seal and prime at the same time. This kind of ground is in fact preferable for acrylic underpainting.

PALETTES The choice of palette is the next important decision. It is a good idea to choose a mixing surface which is the same colour as the primer. The use of brown varnished wooden palettes has become something of a cliché in recent years, and unless the artist is intent on painting into a ground of brown tonality it is unnecessary. The main idea of a palette is that it enables the artist to mix colour on a surface of a similar colour to that of the underpainting or ground. The easiest way to achieve palettes of the chosen colours is to acquire a rectangular sheet of glass and position coloured paper underneath it. As the painting surface changes, the paper may be substituted so that the colours can be mixed in relation to the surface.

It may be useful at first to limit the range of paint colours, and rather than clutter the palette with numerous tints, choose a few key ones from which many others may be mixed. Personal preference and experience will eventually prompt the artist to choose only the colours that are suited to the particular purpose. Although many artists

JANE IN TURBAN
acrylic on canvas

The properties of acrylic paint enable the artist to alter a painting radically, to a greater extent than would be possible even with oils. If, during the course of a painting, the artist feels that the picture has begun badly, rather than proceed reluctantly it is better to reconsider the compositional organization, pose, tonal structure and scale; acrylic allows this type of change.

A canvas support, primed with acrylic primer, makes an ideal base. Acrylic is water-soluble and may be thinned with water during the early stages; later, undiluted, it will give more body.

The model was originally seated on the arm of a couch, wearing a black dress and dark turban (1). The artist chose to depict the subject so that both arms were clearly visible and the head positioned at the top left of the canvas. After establishing the figure, the artist felt that more time and space should be devoted to the head and less to the background (2).

In the second pose the light is coming from the opposite direction. A white turban is substituted to provide more contrast with the shaded background (3). A thin wash partially obscures the first attempt but the canvas is not reprimed so that the first image is clearly visible while the second is being painted (4). The second pose is almost symmetrical, the simple vertical divisions of the background providing three distinct changes of tone. The darkest gives the head and turban emphasis (5).

Another advantage of not repriming the canvas is to allow the first attempt to function as a type of underpainting for the second image. The dark blue, previously used to indicate the dress of the subject, now provides a foundation for the flesh tones that will follow (6). Although acrylic is water-soluble, it can also be mixed with acrylic medium in later stages of the work for more body (7). Flesh tones are applied, using fairly thick paint in cream and pink tints. Because this paint is less fluid than the underpainting, the grain of the canvas picks up the paint as it is lightly dragged over the surface. Acrylic is not water-soluble once it has dried – subsequent layers will not disturb the paint beneath and the technique of application is similar to oil (8).

9

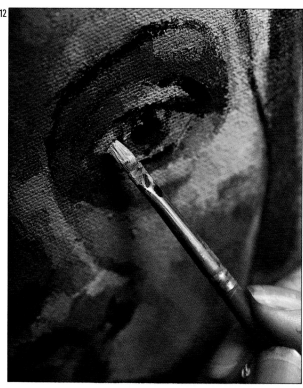

12

13

10

11

As the painting is by now predominantly dark in tonality, application of flesh tones and background washes serves to lighten the picture overall. The dark bands indicating the wall behind the subject are restated in light washes of colour, using shades of green and pink (9). The turban is painted in white and details of the eyes and other features are more clearly defined (10). Each colour on the face is applied as a separate patch, with no attempt to model the colour together. This makes the build-up of form a slow process but each area of the face is gradually brought to the same degree of completion. The artist begins to suggest roughly the outline of a fern in the background (11). As the painting nears its final form, finishing touches in white are applied. The whites of the eyes and highlights are painted (12). A white pearl necklace is added at the last moment, using a simple stipple technique with the point of a brush (13).

In the final painting the last-minute additions of the fern and necklace have served to provide points of focus around the head and alleviate the simpler compositional divisions of the picture. Although the figure is placed squarely on the canvas and fills the picture space, too rigid a symmetry is avoided by placing the fern off-centre at the top. The gentle arc of the chair back and its warm colour serve to complement the curve of the bare arms. Similarly, the pearl necklace echoes in form and colour the white turban framing the face (14).

14

JOANNA
oil and acrylic on canvas

Although some painters favour working 'wet into wet', there are many advantages to making an underpainting. An acrylic underpainting, in particular, may be useful as a means of establishing the image prior to the application of oil. In this portrait, the dominant colour is red; by painting the background first in green, the complementary of red, and then applying red, the final colour has an added vibrancy. Much of the figure is also underpainted in green, in anticipation of the warm skin tones to follow.

An artificial light source was chosen to illuminate the subject and provide a compositional unity.

The chaise-longue allows the model to pose more naturally than would be possible in a straight-backed chair. A folding red screen is chosen for the background, its uniform colour to dominate the tones of the painting and the simple vertical divisions to form an important compositional structure. The spotlight situated to the right of the model lends an element of drama to a straightforward portrait (1).

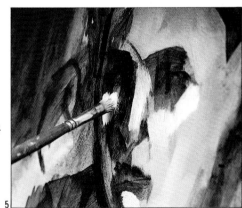

Using washes of green-blue acrylic paint, the artist roughs out the basic structure of the painting, paying little attention to detail but considering the overall design in terms of the abstract relationship of one form to another (2). Lighter shades of green are mixed on the palette (3). These are applied primarily to the face, establishing mid-tones and areas of highlight. The quick-drying property of acrylic paint makes it ideally suited for underpainting; subsequent layers of oil can be applied without hindrance (4 and 5).

Gradually more information about the volume of the form is indicated and the underpainting is left to dry (6). The next stage is to begin painting in oil. Flesh tints are mixed on the palette (7). The skin tones are applied thinly at first to allow the underpainting to show through. The strong light source accentuates the volume of the face (8). The shadow falling across the screen, which defines the space between the subject and background, is darkened (9).

The process of painting should always be able to accommodate change and alteration. Working constantly from the model, the artist revises and refines the angles of the pose (10).

10

11

12

13

An attempt is made to simplify the effect of light on the face so that the painting progresses consistently throughout (11). A soft pink tone is added over the green underpainting of the sweater (12). Detail of the pattern on the scarf is roughed in (13). More attention is paid to the face, particularly the eyes (14).

14

17

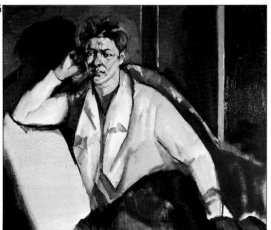

The background is worked up more fully (15). Substantial changes are then made to the face, which becomes more smoothly modelled, and the suggestion of the sofa in the background is painted out, simplifying the composition. The scarf is also reworked (16). In the final version, details such as the glasses and scarf pattern are added. It is always important to consider the negative shapes as positive elements, rather than empty space, to make a strong and unified composition (17).

HUGH SEATED
oil on canvas

The use of oil paint for this portrait enabled the artist to build up layers of paint gradually, incorporating both thick and thin paint. During the early stages of the painting, the figure was positioned against a simple, uniformly coloured backdrop; later on, it was felt that the introduction of another image might accentuate the main subject's pose. To accomplish this, a second figure was introduced, into the background, echoing the leaning posture of the subject.

The figure in the background does not necessarily provide an illusion of depth or indicate recession in space, but has a flatter, more two-dimensional appearance. This intentional ambiguity suggests a painting of a painting directly behind the subject. The use of a picture within a picture is an artistic device often used for emphasis or balance; it is notable in the work of Vermeer and Degas.

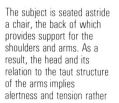

The subject is seated astride a chair, the back of which provides support for the shoulders and arms. As a result, the head and its relation to the taut structure of the arms implies alertness and tension rather than a more conventional, passive pose (1). The initial statement aims at breadth of design rather than detail. After the first white priming, a further priming of pale grey was applied to make the contrast less stark (2).

Working with a limited range of colours, the artist begins by establishing the approximate position of the figure and chair in relation to the shape of the canvas, using paint thinned with turpentine (3). As the model relaxes from the initial pose, more attention can be paid to specific features (4 and 5). Detail is added to the area around the eyes (6). In an attempt to produce a vibrant blue-green background, this area has been underpainted in red. Once the basic forms have been laid in, the picture is left to dry (7). When the painting has dried, small adjustments are made to the shadow areas and contours of the face (8). The blue-green background is applied and further adjustments made to the figure, particularly to the shoulders (9).

More detail is worked into the face, with highlights being applied with a fine brush on the cheeks (10). A fairly strong artificial light source helps to emphasize the form of the face. This is painted in blocks or patches of pigment that are not modelled but are connected as a series of planes. By building the form in this way and continually adapting it, an attempt is made to simplify what in reality is extremely complex (11). The tones of the face are subdued to harmonize with the background colour (12).

A further interpretation of the background is attempted. The properties of oil paint are such that many revisions are possible (13). The asymmetrical position of the figure seems to demand a more complex background and these elements are roughed out in paint (14). By the final stage, the 'picture within the picture' is established in the background and the painting as a whole shows more uniformity of treatment. During the course of the work, considerable alteration has been made to the contours of the head and description of the face (15).

15

YOUNG GIRL
watercolour on paper

Watercolours are used effectively to capture the casual informality of this portrait. Many artists treat watercolours as a way of sketching faces and preparing for later oil paintings, but this picture displays a subtle and detailed use of tones and overlaid colours. The medium is well suited to the representation of a child's smooth, un-wrinkled skin and wispy hair, and to children generally because the layers of quick-drying paint can rapidly be laid one over the other before the subject becomes bored.

The thicker, opaque quality of the shirt is created using a dry-brush technique and the result contrasts with the luminosity of the skin.

Using the thin, pointed end of a round, sable watercolour brush, the lips are painted with precise outlines, partly to emphasize, by contrast, the highlighted area of the upper lip, which is left white (3). Flesh tones are painted in the shadowed areas, reinforcing the eyes, nostrils and chin, while grey is used for darker shadows. The hair is thickened with further layers of paint over the previously dried layers (4).

The outlines of the girl are first drawn in pencil then details of the shape of the eyes and slight shadows around the mouth are painted in grey and burnt umber in thin strokes, the areas left white being as important as those painted. Strands of hair are then added; the brush can usefully be exploited to describe the way the hair moves (1). Well diluted light red and grey shadows under the chin are added, and the shirt filled in with flat grey and blue (2). The paper wrinkles slightly where the washes are well diluted in water to cover the shirt, but this is unimportant as the paper will shrink again as it dries and in any case the wrinkling adds to the texture of the material.

The face and hair are continuously built up with thin layers of brown and grey on dry paint, with highlights on the cheeks left white. Folds in the material are described with strong dark grey lines of shadow, and shadows of the neck also added (5). With attention to detail on the shirt, the artist adds grey paint to show the position of the arms and the creases in the collar, and two thin lines for the lines of stitching (6). When the painting is dry, a brush loaded with dry paint is splayed and drawn across the shirt area to add texture (7). Bright red flowers are painted onto the dried layers of the shirt yoke, and a layer of flesh tones over the lighter cheek finally added, still leaving small patches white for highlights (8).

WOMAN IN DOTTED DRESS
acrylic on canvas

Acrylic is a versatile medium and well suited to the beginner and experienced artist alike. It is particularly useful because it covers well, and if any mistakes are made they can be corrected almost immediately without fear of muddying the colours, or of the mistake showing through. The colours are opaque and vivid, and retain these characteristics for a long time. However, if acrylic paint is applied thinly or is well diluted, it behaves like watercolour, and the colour beneath or the colour of the canvas can in this way be made to show through. This characteristic is valuable when painting flesh, as the translucency commonly associated with skin is usually achieved in paint by layering tones or by allowing a pale ground to show through successive, darker tones.

The subject is seated at a sideways angle to the artist, with her head turned and her eyes looking down (1). On a primed and stretched cotton duck canvas, the artist first sketches in the main contours of the semi-profile, the eyes, nose, chin, jaw, ear and hair, then adds streaks of thin colour and blocks in the hair (2). Concentrating on the face, light flesh tones are filled in over the cheeks, chin, nose and forehead, and small shadows indicate creases of the flesh (3). Rich reds and browns are added to the high cheek area and the forehead, while the area immediately under her eye is left light to show that the light is from above. The lips are given a precise shape and some areas of the chin lightened again with pale, opaque yellows and pinks (4). Grey is laid over the background and the dress filled in with a thin, uniform black wash, so that the red shows through from underneath. The skin of the chest is painted in thin browns and the white priming shows through, giving it a luminous quality (5).

The dress is built up with further strokes of thin black paint applied with a broad brush and the basic shadows of the arm and shoulder are added. Further flesh tones are painted on the neck and chest to describe the shape of the collarbones and the ear is filled with shadows using a thin brush. White, yellow and red dots are stencilled over the black in thick, opaque paint (6). Rows of dots are applied with a thin brush using stencils of different sizes. Sometimes the artist encroaches into the background, but this abstract quality adds interest to the painting (7). Some of the dots are built up freehand (8). The dress is covered with these dots at different angles and in different colours (9).

ADDIE
gouache on paper

The fluidity of water-based paints such as gouache means that they are ideally suited for making either colour studies, in preparation for larger oil paintings, or quick, complete pictures when time is limited. This type of paint is usually regarded, however, as better suited to landscape subjects than faces and some experimentation will be necessary when attempting to render the solidity of the human figure and the precise values of skin tones.

Water-soluble paints are best applied to stretched paper to prevent the paint wrinkling the paper as it dries. The paper should be prepared by wetting it thoroughly on both sides and then attaching it to a drawing board with strips of gummed paper around the perimeter. When the paper dries it will shrink slightly; subsequently it is ready for the application of paint.

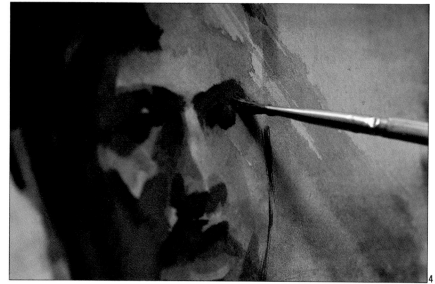

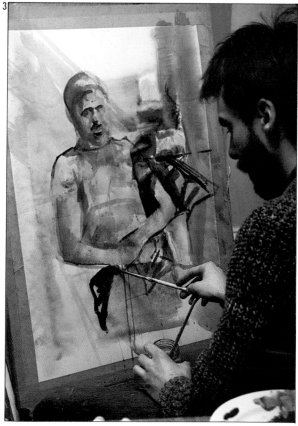

The pose of the model, although symmetrical from the front, appears slightly turned to one side when seen from the artist's viewpoint. Natural light from a window to the right of the model illuminates the form (1). The artist begins by drawing with the brush rather than making a preliminary pencil sketch (2 and 3). This method allows more freedom to convey the effects of light, especially on the face (4). The painting grows out of the drawing rather than being considered as a separate activity from the initial statement. The paint is kept as fluid as possible (5).

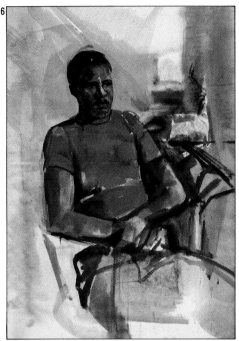

Gouache always remains water-soluble, unlike acrylic paint which is also water-based. The application of wet paint over dry may disturb and mix with the preceding colour. This need not be a disadvantage, if a fluid result is required. Here the area surrounding the figure is conveyed by overlapping washes of colour

(6). The bulk of the figure is indicated in a broad painterly treatment. The positions of areas of paint are considered with respect to their abstract qualities within the rectangle of the surface as well as their more obvious representational associations (7). The structure of the head is continually assessed and reassessed during the course

of the work. By the final stage, the earlier, more approximate statement has been subtly altered. More time is spent painting the face – the focus of interest for the portraitist – than any other part of the picture (8).

Selection and composition

The process of selection involved in drawing or painting a portrait is of paramount importance to the artist, and as well as selecting the particular medium it is important that the artist is able to select the most essential qualities of pose and structure and present them in terms of a pictorial composition. However complex the posture of the figure may appear at first glance, it can always be simplified in relation to the relative positions of the individual forms. In attempting to draw the face it is important to consider the angle of the neck and shoulders even if they will not be evident in the final picture. At every point of articulation the axis changes direction and it is necessary to understand these changes and how they affect the distribution of weight in the figure as a whole.

Before beginning to draw or paint a portrait, a position should be established and the board or canvas placed to allow an easy view of both the surface and the model without too much unnecessary movement. In art schools students often sit astride a wooden seat known as a 'donkey'. This comprises a wooden support for both the artist and the drawing board or canvas. A chair or easel may be used but if a table is preferred it is important that the support is not resting horizontally or distortion will occur due to the shortened angle of the paper. If the artist is seated with the board or canvas just resting and easily moved, the horizontal edge of the surface may be related to any parallel equivalents in the subject. This system only works, however, if the board or canvas is positioned directly in front of the artist in such a way that, to the artist, the developing image appears to be directly below his or her view of the model. If the model is seated on a chair against a wall an indication of the floor level at the base of the wall can be established as a horizontal line. If this appears to be parallel to the top edge of the board or canvas, then a vertical axis can also be established and a constant movement of the eye between the surface and the model will enable the artist to establish the structure quite easily. Many artists use a plumb line as a vertical measure. Personal preference dictates to what degree these devices are employed.

In many instances the subject will not include obvious geometric divisions and it is then useful to situate the model in such a way that some architectural element is visible. This could be a window frame or a doorway or even a table, allowing the artist to observe negative shapes between the form of the figure and the surrounding space. Many attempts at drawing and painting do not consider the figure in relation to its immediate environment, and a common misconception arises whereby the figure is considered to be as important as the surroundings are unimportant. Once aware of the use of relating the figure to the background, the idea of composition becomes increasingly evident.

The idea of drawing as design, which includes the idea of drawing with a brush, involves the ability to consider the image in relation to the shape and format of the surface. During the Renaissance, paintings were often incorporated

LEFT **Clementine Ogilvy, Lady Spencer-Churchill**, Sir John Lavery (1856 - 1941). This charming picture is thought to have been painted while the artist was staying with the Churchills at Hoe Farm, Godalming, in about 1915. It is interesting to consider how the portrait would have looked without the foreground table and the objects on it, as they provide this composition with the necessary solidity of a right-angle. The whole picture forms an elongated right-angled triangle, the top of the window and Lady Spencer-Churchill's feet forming the other angles. Her body provides an elegant curve within the main shape, while the vertical points of the cushions and the child's head add interest to the surface structure.

ABOVE The human figure is capable of an infinite number of movements, and when composing a portrait it is worth considering not only how to pose the subject but how to place the pose within the shape of the paper, board or canvas. The whole figure could be included, or just a section. The figure could be placed centrally or to one side, with some of it outside the frame. While selecting and planning in this way, the artist should be considering the emotional responses of the spectator to particular poses and to resulting surface structures. RIGHT While searching for a suitable pose and a pleasing angle from which to view it, the artist can sketch the figure in possible positions. Chalk and charcoal are suited to this purpose.

into architectural settings and predetermined shapes affected the pictorial design. The use of a rectangular support for painting and drawing has a long tradition and is still popular because it is convenient. The shape will affect the nature of the image: if the subject involves any horizontal or vertical divisions they can be related to the boundaries of the paper and so provide a form of visual echo which will give the drawing a stability and unity. Circular, square or irregularly shaped surfaces demand different compositional considerations, but can be used to good effect.

A common method of planning the structure of a work involves subdividing a sheet of paper into smaller rectangles and making quick drawings. In this way many different compositional structures may be found within a seemingly limited subject. By contemplating the various pictorial options, the artist will be able to exercise control and eliminate the arbitrary arrangement that would probably be the result of a lack of consideration. The acknowledgement of negative shapes will become second nature if they are considered from the start. Although there is a natural temptation to focus on the face,

a pictorial unity will only emerge through a more general awareness of the space occupied by and around the figure.

One of the easier ways to consider the organization of material can be to cut a rectangle out of a piece of card and view the subject through it. By moving it horizontally and vertically the figure may be considered in different positions within the rectangle. By moving the card nearer to the figure the area of space around the figure decreases and eventually the face will appear to fill the whole frame. Although the window frame idea may be dispensed with, the activity of looking and selecting will at some point involve making a mental note of the imaginary boundaries of the sheet of paper, or to the intended boundaries within the sheet. It is common practice to position the portrait in the centre of the paper and proceed outwards from the centre, and yet a more interesting configuration may result by considering other, more unusual positions within the rectangle. The ease with which many great artists have used compositional devices is deceptively subtle and, needless to say, such deception is the product of

RIGHT **A Memory/Our Dear Stan** (1976), Anthony Green. The charm of this portrait is that the artist has treated an ordinary looking subject and setting with a care and consideration that betrays his feelings. Although the man is viewed mowing his lawn in a setting which thousands recognize as similar to their own home, the shape of the canvas is unique and only allows the man's house and garden to be described, as if he exists in a world of his own.

Framing

The artist can select the frame best suited to the composition and the desired effect by using two L-shaped pieces of paper or cardboard and moving them to extend or shorten the edges. Using an instant photograph to help in composing the picture, the whole shot of this intended scene shows some empty floor space, an expanse of door and the arm of another model across the bed (1). Treated in a vertical format the girl's face seems longer (2). It is possible to concentrate on the face by ignoring all surrounding objects and details, leaving the background empty and making the face fill the frame (3), but the figure and the mirror behind are finally included in the chosen frame to add interest (4). Mirrors can be used effectively in portraits as they automatically show two sides of the subject and allow the spectator to glimpse something of the rest of the artist's view.

ABOVE Ingres' masterful exploitation of the canvas surface can be seen in this line drawing taken from **Monsieur Bertin.** The bulkiness of the figure, the way the head sinks into the shoulders and the heavy, round back of the chair all give an impression of solidity, which is enhanced by the low placement of the half-figure within the frame. It is a strong, triangular composition, designed to express something of the subject's character and to force the viewer's response.

considerable knowledge and experience. The idea of composition has so far been considered in formal terms but an awareness of compositional structure can also affect the mood of the drawing by the psychological implications of the positioning of the figure.

During the Renaissance compositional organization provided the foundation for all artistic concerns, and the rediscovery of a means of establishing ideal proportions resulted in a general belief in the importance of the golden section. This term is applied to the aesthetic harmony of proportion produced when a line is divided in such a way that the smaller division relates to the larger just as the larger relates to the whole. By geometric application, a rectangle can also be constructed in such a way that subdivisions within the rectangle will accord with this harmonious relationship. Although some painters have put this theoretical concern into strict practice, many others have applied it in an intuitive manner. Triangles and pyramids have also been employed as a means of establishing a

stable and powerful structure, one especially evident in religious compositions. With experience, painters have taken more liberties with pictorial organization, and it may not be evident that any one geometric form dominates compositional structure through the centuries.

When Ingres drew or painted a male figure he invariably used an upright and alert posture, and the conscious positioning was often echoed by the positions of surrounding objects or by patterns. Similarly, when drawing or painting a portrait of a woman he would accentuate the curvature of the body in the surrounding clothing and drapery. The compositional organization of his portraits reflects the respective roles of men and women in society.

In the twentieth century Henri Matisse explored this kind of pictorial association to such a degree that the repetition of curves in his compositions become a dominant feature of his work. Both Ingres and Matisse were aware that hard angular forms evoke strength and severity while the repetition of curves often evokes the

Contrasting viewpoints
Matisse, a member of the Fauves group of painters, is famous for his bright, emotive use of colour which he often exploited for strong, decorative effects. These two portraits, **Study of Madame Matisse, (far left)** and **Portrait of Derain (left)** look quite different from their originals when seen in black-and-white reproduction because the colour is essential to their feeling of vibrancy and liveliness; without the distraction of Matisse's colour, however, they usefully illustrate the artist's deliberate exploitation of space. For his wife's portrait, he chose to stand at a distance to allow a view of her whole figure and her surroundings, so adding an aura of domesticity and comfort, while the beauty of the scene outside, bathed in sunlight, is also imparted. These things provide reasons for, and enhance, her obvious enjoyment of the situation. For Derain, Matisse wanted an uncluttered view, and a strong and direct portrait is the result.

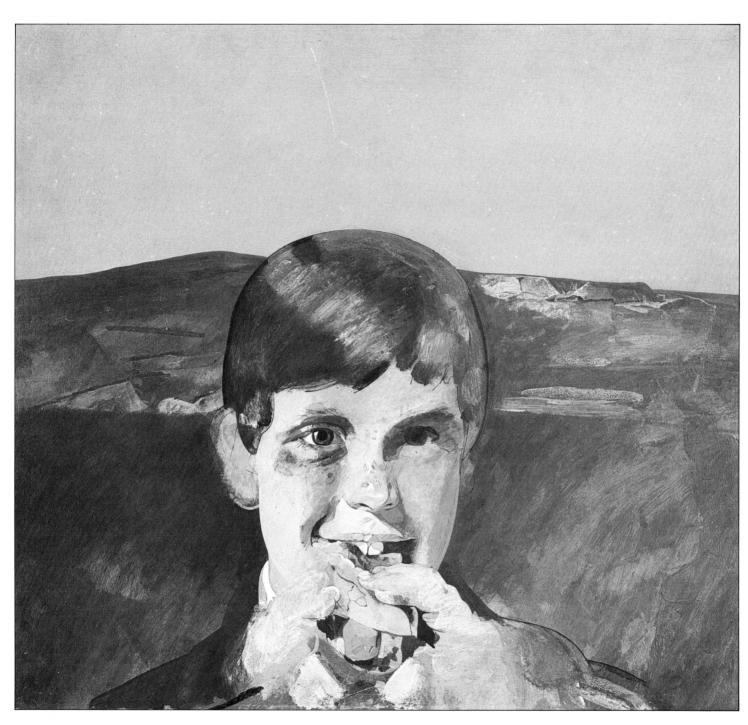

quite different sensations of sensuality or gentleness.

One of Ingres' most successful male portraits is *Monsieur Bertin*. The huge bulk of the man's body provides a formidable appearance, and although the composition cannot be equated to any single geometric form, its underlying structure forms a triangle. The feeling of weight pressing on the thighs by the hands is accentuated by their being at the lower edge of the painting. Nothing about the composition is ar-

bitrary; the calculated area of space above the head provides a contrast to the tightly compact volume of the lower portion of the picture. At first glance it might be assumed that the powerful image is due to the facial expression but, like many powerful portraits, the feeling of human presence is accentuated by the thoughtful pictorial structure.

Composition has been considered so far in two-dimensional terms and although the surface structure is crucial to the success of a picture, it

prompts a further consideration of structure in a three-dimensional sense. In *Monsieur Bertin*, it is evident that the bulk of the figure can be considered in relation to its depth. Several existing studies for this picture reveal how Ingres considered alternative postures and had originally intended the figure to be standing. Had Ingres incorporated the whole figure within the picture, the powerful effect would have been diminished. The positioning of the figure in relation to the perimeter of the canvas is crucial.

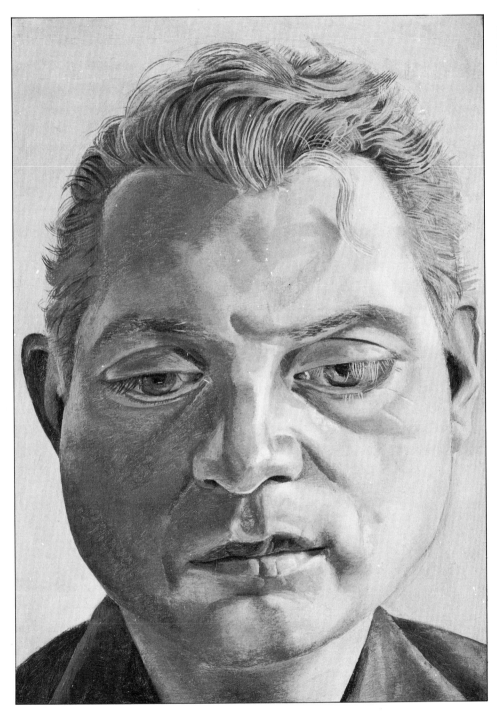

Lucian Freud is a contemporary painter who has exploited the psychological tensions made possible through pictorial organization. The results are often inventive and surprising, and few recent painters have been able to produce such striking images within an orthodox format. In the portrait of Francis Bacon the intensity of the image is due partly to the microscopic attention to detail and partly to the simple compositional compactness. Nothing interferes with the frank description of the face and yet the choice of such a small area of space around the head suggests an awareness of the positive effect it would have. The tension in this picture occurs because of the relationship between the tangible volume of the face, which seems to expand outwards, and the abrupt perimeter of the rectangle which presses inwards and contains the image.

Before considering the activity of painting it is worth emphasizing that the compositional structure in a drawing or painting involves selecting the positions of certain objects or features which may be considered in terms of lines and shapes within the whole. In order to find those shapes it is first necessary to select the objects or props required. In both the above examples the human form is the focus of interest. Both Ingres and Lucian Freud chose to isolate their subjects by carefully considering and limiting the area of surface not occupied by the figure. In many other instances Lucian Freud juxtaposes his figure with either an animal, a plant or some aspect of a domestic interior. Ingres, on the other hand, presented his subjects with certain attributes of social status and went to great lengths to find the right accessories for his portraits; he also placed an emphasis on clothing and jewellery. From this, it would be reasonable to assume that he spent a considerable amount of time selecting and organizing his subjects in terms of colour and texture, as well as shape.

By looking at any portrait painter of any period it will be apparent that each one found a personal way of selecting from the numerous possibilities evident in reality. It is often easier to start with a simple format of one figure situated against a simple background. With experience it may be possible to gradually involve other objects that reveal clues about the identity of the sitter. These may take the form of a direct reference to the sitter's occupation or personal interest; alternatively they may simply suggest an interior space, for example, a domestic environment. Many painters have used landscape backgrounds for portraits or a combination of both interior and exterior by the use of a window. The possibilities are endless and yet every given situation demands a similar understanding of the relationship between the shape of the figure and the surroundings. The more complex subjects probably involve more preparatory work and it is often necessary to draw the various components of the subject separately having considered the whole. Written notes on colour

ABOVE LEFT **Boy Eating a Hot Dog** (1960 - 65), Peter Blake. In this portrait, Blake seems to be summing up the transience not only of movement but of youth. The boy obviously relishes the hot dog; Blake painted it with emphasis and placed it in the centre foreground but, surrounded by teeth and about to be consumed, the

existence of the hot dog makes a direct play on the fleeting qualities of energy and life, and dramatically points out the conflict between the fact that paintings last while situations do not.
ABOVE **Francis Bacon**, Lucian Freud. The confrontation between subject and spectator has been forced by

the fact that the face takes up the entire surface of this picture. The meticulous detail of the features, skin and hair matches the close viewpoint, but the subject is looking down as if to retain a certain privacy. There is a sympathy between the subject and the artist, expressed in the gentleness of expression.

and lighting may be useful when it comes to translating the image into a painting; photographs can also be used to provide the information that cannot always be gained during the limited time available with a model.

Any appraisal of the elements of compositional structure would be incomplete without some comment on the work of Edgar Degas. His ability to depict figures in natural and unforced poses has rarely been equalled. Degas managed to push the boundaries of portraiture further than any previous artist, and his inventive results are the product of a lifelong fascination with the problems of pictorial organization. The in-

fluence of photography and the Japanese print directly affected Degas' attitude to composition. He realized that in reality a figure or group rarely occupies a position that would be consistent with the commonly accepted poses in orthodox portraiture. In order to convey a more convincing posture Degas would deliberately choose odd angles for his viewpoint. By looking from above, the figure would adopt more unusual shapes in relation to the rectangle. By positioning the figure close to the edge of the canvas and emphasizing the large areas of empty space, Degas was able to suggest a degree of informality almost unprecedented in Western art.

BELOW **The Meeting** or **Good Day Monsieur Courbet** (1854), Gustave Courbet. The supposed position of the spectator is below the subjects of this group portrait and also to one side; in fact he or she would be standing on the grass verge. Courbet in this way makes the spectator feel apart from the situation, like an onlooker, a **voyeur**. This technique indicates Courbet's arrogance.

RIGHT **Portrait of Diego Martelli**, Edgar Degas. Influenced by the unusual perspective of Japanese prints, Degas approached this portrait from above, exploiting the viewpoint to emphasize the squatness of the man's figure. To place the figure deliberately to one side of the picture and to include a large expanse of table-top, was considered almost revolutionary in the mid-nineteenth century.

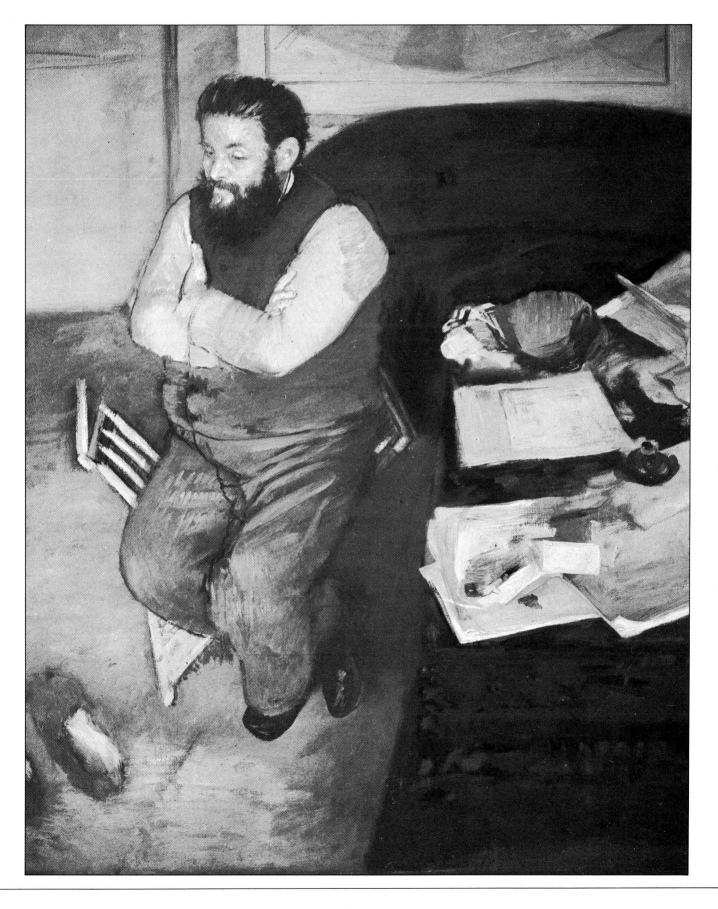

INDEX

Page numbers in *italic* refer to the illustrations and their captions.

R

S

CONTRIBUTORY ARTISTS

Key:
(l) left; (r) right; (t) top; (b) bottom; (c) centre.

Margaret Clarke
92-3, 96-9, 126-9

Terence Clark
94-5

John Devane
49, 55(tr), 58-9, 78, 90-1, 102-3, 130-3, 134-7, 142-3, 145(b)

Bill Dare
55(tc)

Clive Howard
100-1

Ian Sidaway
138-9, 140-1

Stan Smith
55(tl), (bl), (br), 73(t), 77(r), 82, 83

Mark Winer
71(r)

ACKNOWLEDGEMENTS

The illustrations on these pages were reproduced by courtesy of the following:

6, 7, 8, 9 (l) the Trustees, The National Gallery, London; 9(r) the Greater London Council as Administrative Trustee of the Iveagh Bequest, Kenwood House; 10 Prado, Madrid; 11(t) Courtauld Institute Galleries, London; 11(b) the Trustees, The British Museum, London; 12(t) (Ronald Sheridan's Photo Library); 12(b) Nigel Osborne; 13 Uffizi, Florence; 14 Gemäldegalerie, Staatliche Museen, West Berlin; 15 the Trustees, The National Gallery, London; 16, 17 Uffizi, Florence; 18 The National Gallery of Art, Washington D.C.; 19, 20 Louvre, Paris; 21 The Metropolitan Museum of Art, New York, Robert Lehman Collection, 1975; 22 the Trustees, The National Gallery, London; 23 Louvre, Paris; 24, 25 The Metropolitan Museum of Art, Bequest of Mrs H.O. Havemeyer, 1929; 26 the Trustees, The National Gallery, London; 27 Prado, Madrid; 28 Frans Halsmuseum, Haarlem; 29 the Trustees, The National Gallery, London; 30 Mauritshuis, The Hague; 31, 32, 33(l) the Trustees, The National Gallery, London; 33(r) Musées Royaux des Beaux-Arts, Brussels; 34(l) the Trustees, The Wallace Collection, London; 34(r) the Trustees, The National Gallery, London; 35 Louvre, Paris; 36(t) Louvre, Paris (Bridgeman Art Library); 36(b) Musée du Jeu-de-Paume; 38 the Trustees, The National Gallery, London; 41 The Metropolitan Museum of Art, New York, Bequest of Gertrude Stein, 1946 ©SPADEM; 42(t) Petersburg Press ©David Hockney 1973; 42(b) The Tate Gallery, London; 43 The Tate Gallery, London ©Waddington Galleries, London; 44 QED Publishing; 45 (Fotomas Index); 46, 47 Quarto Publishing; 48 (Fotomas Index); 50 Quarto Publishing; 51 the Trustees, The British Museum, London (John Freeman); 52 The Metropolitan Museum of Art, New York, Bequest of Joseph Pulitzer, 1924; 53(r) Accademia, Venice (Scala); 60 reproduced by gracious permission of Her Majesty the Queen; 61 the Trustees, The National Gallery, London; 62 Albertina, Vienna; 63(l) The National Portrait Gallery, London; 63(r) the Trustees, The British Museum, London; 64-5 Musées Royaux des Beaux-Arts, Brussels; 66,67 the Trustees, The National Gallery, London; 71(l) Gemeentemuseum, The Hague, Collection Haags ©SPADEM; 72 Petersburg Press ©David Hockney 1973; 73(l) Biblioteca Marucelliana, Florence; 74 reproduced by gracious permission of Her Majesty the Queen; 75 the Trustees, The British Museum, London; 76 The Arts Council of Great Britain; 77(l) The Tate Gallery, London ©ADAGP; 79 Louvre, Paris; 80(l) private collection, London ©SPADEM; 80(r) The Tate Gallery, London; 81 the Trustees, The British Museum, London; 84 Glasgow Museums and Art Galleries, The Burrell Collection; 85 Chicago Art Institute; 86 Petersburg Press ©David Hockney 1976; 87 Marlborough Fine Art, London; 88 The National Portrait Gallery, London; 89(tl) Michael ffolkes, Punch Magazine; 89(tr) Richard Cole; 89(bl) The National Portrait Gallery, London; 89(br) Faber and Faber, London; 104(l) the Trustees, The British Museum, London; 104 (r) The National Gallery of Art, Washington D.C., Mellon Collection; 105 Uffizi, Florence; 106(tl) Louvre, Paris; 106(bl), (r), 107, 108 the Trustees, The National Gallery, London; 109 Uffizi, Florence; 110(l), (r), 111 the Trustees, The National Gallery, London; 113(l) The Wellington Museum, London; 113(r), 114(l), (r), 115 the Trustees, The National Gallery, London; 116(tl) The National Portrait Gallery, London; 116(tr) Louvre, Paris; 116(bl) The Tate Gallery, London; 116(br) Louvre, Paris; 117 Birmingham Museum and Art Gallery; 118(l) The National Portrait Gallery, London; 118(r) Walker Art Gallery, Liverpool; 119(t) Marlborough Fine Art, London; 119(b) The Tate Gallery, London ©Anthony d'Offay Gallery, London; 121 The Tate Gallery, London ©ADAGP; 123(tl), (tr) the Trustees, The National Gallery, London; 123(b) The Tate Gallery, London; 124(cl) Home House Society Trustees, Courtauld Institute Galleries, London; 124(cr) The Tate Gallery ©David Hockney 1970; 125 Anthony Green; 144 The National Portrait Gallery, London; 146 Anthony Green; 148 private collection, Switzerland ©SPADEM; 149 The Tate Gallery, London ©SPADEM; 150 The Arts Council of Great Britain; 151 The Tate Gallery, London; 152 Musée Fabre, Montpellier; 153 The National Gallery of Scotland, Edinburgh.

Key:
(l) left; (r) right; (t) top; (b) bottom; (c) centre.